SHACKLETON'S BOAT

THE STORY OF THE
JAMES CAIRD

HARDING MCGREGOR DUNNETT (1909–2000) grew up mainly in South London. He was a pupil at Dulwich College when the *James Caird* first arrived there. His interest continued throughout the years and, besides writing this book, it led him to found **The James Caird Society** to perpetuate the memory of Shackleton's heroic achievements and the boat which served him so well.

www.jamescairdsociety.com

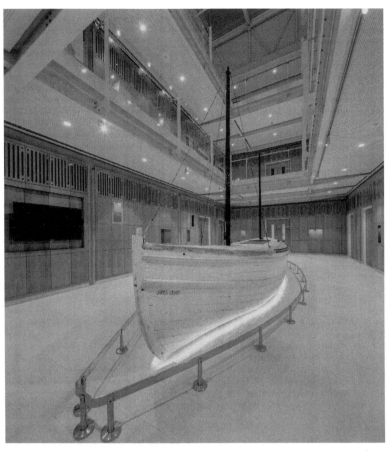

The *James Caird* displayed in its spacious new home, the James Caird Hall of The Laboratory, the newly opened science building at Shackleton's old school, Dulwich College. Shackleton was a day boy at Dulwich from 1887–1890, from the age of thirteen.

SHACKLETON'S BOAT

THE STORY OF THE
JAMES CAIRD

HARDING McGREGOR DUNNETT

The Collins Press

PUBLISHED IN 2015 BY
The Collins Press
West Link Park
Doughcloyne
Wilton
Cork

First published in hardback in 1996 by Neville & Harding, UK

Paperback ISBN: 978-1-84889-212-5
PDF eBook ISBN: 978-1-84889-491-4
EPUB eBook ISBN: 978-1-84889-492-1
Kindle ISBN: 978-1-84889-493-8

Design and typesetting by Burns Design
Typeset in Sabon
Printed in Dublin by Sprintprint

CONTENTS

It is now nearly twenty years since Harding Dunnett, Founder and first Chairman of The James Caird Society, published this impressive book. How appropriate it should be reissued in this, the second of the three Shackleton Centenary years, celebrating Ernest Shackleton's Imperial Trans-Antarctic Expedition; with particular reference to *Endurance*, the ship of the Weddell Sea Expedition but not forgetting *Aurora*, the ship of the Ross Sea Party.

The voyage of the tiny *James Caird* (one of *Endurance*'s three lifeboats) is the stuff of dreams. Not quite 23ft (6.5m), the *James Caird* voyaged in winter across 800 miles of the stormiest seas in the world, the Southern Ocean. Conditions

The Hon. Alexandra Shackleton

on board were appalling; finding South Georgia was due to the miraculous navigation of Frank Worsley, who located this tiny speck in the ocean. The story does not end there: Shackleton and his companions Crean and Worsley then had to traverse the unmapped mountainous interior of South Georgia.

Finally, after four attempts, Shackleton with the help of the Chilean navy in August 1916 brought rescue to the twenty-two men stranded on Elephant Island. This has been described as one of the greatest rescues in history.

The 'Shackleton Double' was not successfully recreated until 2013 by Tim Jarvis, leader of the Shackleton Epic Expedition. Their boat (named after myself as Patron) was accurate, to all but a quarter of an inch.

Over the years I have taken part in a great many Shackleton events, both in Ireland and further afield. Amongst the most memorable were opening the superb Shackleton Exhibition at Dulwich College in 2000, and meeting the victorious Shackleton Epic team in South Georgia in 2013.

The fascinating detail of the building of the *James Caird* contained in this book provided vital information in the Shackleton Epic Expedition's search for authenticity. In an attempt to get closer to the spirit of Shackleton, Tim and his men wore similar clothing and navigated by the stars and attempted (!) to eat similar food. Their traverse of South Georgia took around ninety hours in contrast to Ernest Shackleton's thirty-six!

So the story lives on; I think Harding Dunnett would have been pleased.

Alexandra Shackleton

THE HON. ALEXANDRA SHACKLETON

The saga of Shackleton's many exploits as an Antarctic explorer might well be fiction rather than fact. The man and his deeds seem larger than life and none ranks higher than the epic of the *James Caird*.

Others have written biographies of the man and described that remarkable boat journey but, until now, no book has concentrated exclusively on the story of the boat, her construction and rig, her journeys, her return to England in 1919 and then her vicissitudes, which continued until the present day. These are as varied as the life of the man who sailed her, and should not go unrecorded. The anniversary of that outstanding feat of seamanship in the *James Caird* would seem to be an appropriate occasion to do so.

I had become involved with the *James Caird* through my connections with Dulwich College as schoolboy and alumnus. Several years ago I produced a small book entitled *Eminent Alleynians*, consisting of short biographical notes about a number of distinguished former pupils. Shackleton

Dulwich College in Shackleton's time

topped the list. A few years later, when the *James Caird* returned from the National Maritime Museum to Dulwich, I offered to compile a script for a video programme about Shackleton's Boat Journey, for the instruction of successive generations of boys. This was produced 'in house', with the enthusiastic co-operation of John Bardell, a science master. The connection with Dulwich continued to develop when I persuaded several other enthusiasts to help launch The James Caird Society, to commemorate Shackleton and his achievements. The Society has grown rapidly since its inception in May 1994 and is already attracting international support.

In the preparation of *Eminent Alleynians*, the video and now this book, I am indebted to many at Dulwich College for help and encouragement, but especially to Margaret Slythe, then Head of Library and Archivist, for sharing her invaluable fund of knowledge and experience of the subject, her wise guidance, for all the fun we had in the hunt and for so many acts of kindness that I have lost count of them. I also have to thank Anthony Verity, then Master of the College, for realising the value of lending the *James Caird* to the London International Boat Show in 1994, and welcoming the proposal for a James Caird Society; John Bardell for his photographic and electronic wizardry, his skill in producing the video, and unstinting help in every emergency; Bob Alexander, Clerk to the Governors, for supplying details of the trials and tribulations of the *James Caird* since the 1920s; and Will Skinner, former Bursar, for acting, perforce, as banker to The James Caird Society in its salad days.

I take this opportunity to thank the Trans-Antarctic Association, and particularly the Honorary Secretary at the time, Dr Peter Clarkson, for providing a grant towards the cost of producing the Shackleton video; also members of staff at the National Maritime Museum who were most helpful at that time, as were the library staff at the Scott Polar Research Institute. I am very grateful to the Institute for permission to use extracts from Worsley's diary and to reproduce his log of the Boat Journey.

Most of the photographs have come from the archives of Dulwich College and my thanks go to Dr Jan Piggott, the Archivist, for permission to use them. Other sources are listed separately. I am especially in debt to Daphne Courtney Taylor for preparing the drawings and diagrams used in the Shackleton video, some of which are reproduced here. I wish to thank David Emms, formerly Master of Dulwich College, and once more, Margaret Slythe, for their most helpful comments on the text. Angus Erskine cast an eagle eye over a set of galley proofs and I am greatly indebted to his deep knowledge and personal experience of the subject.

Sir Vivian Fuchs most kindly contributed the Foreword for the original edition of this book. His memorable expedition in 1955–58, when he completed what his predecessor, Shackleton, set out to do in 1914, inevitably poses the question, could Shackleton, with dog teams only, have managed to complete a crossing of the Antarctic continent?

My sincere thanks and appreciation go to The Hon. Alexandra Shackleton for adding a Shackleton imprimatur to my efforts. From the day she joined us on the Boat Show display, her enthusiasm and energies have never flagged, and later, her contribution, as its very active President, to the success of The James Caird Society is beyond reckoning. The Shackleton strain has not failed the third generation.

One man whom I cannot overlook is Trevor Potts. If he had not bulldozed his 'In the Wake of Shackleton' expedition past all the forces that tried to stop him building his replica of the *James Caird*, and sailing his *Sir Ernest Shackleton* from Elephant Island to South Georgia, I doubt whether the *James Caird* would ever have graced the Boat Show, or that the need for The James Caird Society would have emerged. So full marks to Trevor: he had no idea what a spin-off his efforts would have.

I owe more than I can express to Anthony and Vanessa Harvey for their endless generosity and many acts of kindness, and for their enthusiasm and inspiration over a number of years, and I offer my sincere thanks to both of them.

Finally, I must emphasise how much I owe to the unstinting support and encouragement of my family, particularly when the *James Caird* was displayed at the Boat Show and later, in helping to make The James Caird Society a success. I owe more to my daughters, Pippa Hare, Honorary Secretary of the Society and Virginia Woodrow, for practical help with administration than I can express; likewise to my son, Roderic Harding McGregor Dunnett, for help with the preparation of my manuscript for publication, at the proof-reading stage and to my wife, Monica, for putting up with a husband who, in all reason, should have given up these activities years ago. To all of them I offer my heartfelt thanks for much else besides.

Harding Dunnett

Harding McGregor Dunnett was born on 20 March 1909. He and his twin brother, Valentine, were at school at Dulwich College from 1922–1926. During that time the 23-foot whaler, the *James Caird*, was donated to the school in memory of Sir Ernest Shackleton, who had been at the college from 1887–90.

Harding, who spent his working life in public relations and exhibition design, rediscovered Shackleton whilst writing a book on eminent old boys of Dulwich College. This jogged his memory of the boat, 'the Boss' and his supreme leadership qualities, which have since been used as a yardstick, particularly in the field of industry.

In 1986 Harding, with the then archivist Margaret Slythe, set about bringing the restored *James Caird* back to Dulwich from the Greenwich Maritime Museum. It was installed in the College's North Cloister and can now be seen displayed in the James Caird Hall of the new Science Laboratory. Soon after, with the aid of Physics Master John Bardell, Harding produced a very effective home-grown video of the story of the *James Caird*.

In 1994 Trevor Potts mounted his 'In the Wake of Shackleton' expedition to re-enact Shackleton's boat journey. Harding, in his element, took on the role of press officer for the expedition. At the same time the *James Caird* was displayed at the London Boat Show, with Harding and his family manning the stand. A few months later the James Caird Society was formed and in 1996 Harding published his book, *Shackleton's Boat*, dealing exclusively with the *James Caird* and its remarkable history. Harding's 'finding' of Shackleton, late in his life, allowed him to bring all his PR experience, talent and good humour to bear on the subject.

Harding Dunnett photographed beside Shackleton's grave at Grytviken

This book and a thriving James Caird Society, now more than two decades old, are his legacy to the world. Harding died on 22 April 2000, having made it, as he hoped, into the new millennium.

GINNY WOODROW

ACKNOWLEDGEMENTS

In the text, I have quoted freely from Shackleton's *South* and wish to thank the Shackleton family for permission to do so. My thanks go to The Tower Hamlets Local History Librarian for locating the boatyard of W. & J. Leslie, builders of the *James Caird*.

Many others including Patrick Walcot, and Terry Walsh of the Alleyn Club, have helped in a variety of ways during the long gestation period of this book to whom I can only offer a general vote of thanks.

ILLUSTRATIONS

The majority of the illustrations have been supplied from the Dulwich College Archives, with the kind permission of the Archivist, Dr J. R. Piggott and the Acting Master Chris Field. I am also indebted to the following institutions and individuals for permission to use illustrations in their possession:

Dulwich College: p. ii.

The James Caird Society: p. vi.

Virginia Woodrow: p. xii, p. 144 (bottom right) and for designing the maps on pp 5, 40 and 48 (bottom).

Estate of Harding Dunnett: p. xiii.

The National Maritime Museum: pp. 3 (right), 157 (both) and159 (both).

The Royal Geographical Society: pp. 6 (both) and 19 (right).

University of St Andrews Library: p. 9 (middle).

Mrs Patricia Ducé: p. 12.

Val Dunnett: p. 16 (top).

Hodder Headline: p. 20 (left).

Dundee Central Library: p. 21.

Kristoffer Wegger: p. 23.

James Meiklejohn and his Norwegian ex-whaling associates: pp. 29, 116 (top) and 118 (top).

Dr Peter Clarkson and Dr Roger Clayton: pp. 31 (top), 105, 108, 109 (top), 110, 114 (top) and 115 (top).

Daphne Courtney Taylor: pp. 78 (both), 88, 89 (both), 90, 91 (top), 93, 95, 97 (both), 99, 114 (bottom) and 117 (bottom).

The Scott Polar Research Institute: p. 91 (bottom).

Angus Erskine: pp. 106, 109 (bottom) and 115 (bottom).

Richard Hudson: p. 129.

Tony Hunt: p. 130.

H. E. J. Evans: p. 134 (top).

Mrs Jean Macklin: p. 141 (bottom).

Norsk Polarinstitutt: p. 143 (top).

Con Collins: p. 144 (top left).

The British Antarctic Survey: p. 144 (top right).

Crown Agent Stamp Bureau: p. 146.

An Old Alleynian: p. 153 (top).

The late C. Walter Hodges: p. 150.

Mrs Pippa Hare: pp. 177 and 178 (bottom).

I have been unable to trace the owners of several of the illustrations. If I have omitted to make due acknowledgement for any I hereby offer my apologies.

ANTARCTICA

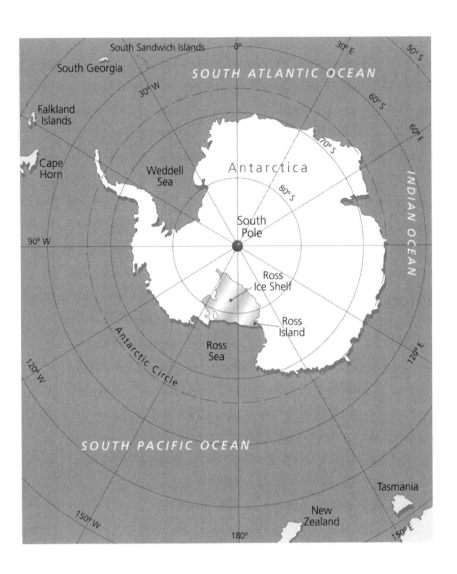

PRELUDE TO A LEGEND

*O*n a quiet countrified part of south London, sheltering in the cloister of a famous school of ancient lineage, resting on a bed of grey South Atlantic boulders, is a small boat, painted white and ketch-rigged, with all sails set.

Undoubtedly the most famous small boat in existence, she has been displayed at the school, off and on, since 1924. Yet the schoolboys jostle past her day in day out, with hardly a glance. She is a part of their everyday existence.

Yet for visitors who make the pilgrimage from distant places, such as Australia, New Zealand, Canada, the United States and Scandinavia, to see her, as well as from many parts of Britain, she is more than a boat: she is an icon, a marvel, a stimulus to the imagination.

In 1916, this small boat played a vital part in an incredible journey which saved the lives of 28 ship-wrecked men. She epitomises, perhaps better than any other existing artefact, the extraordinary qualities of the man who led the expedition and masterminded the rescue.

The man was Sir Ernest Shackleton, the boat is the *James Caird*, and the school, Shackleton's alma mater, Dulwich College. The date of the voyage was April to May 1916.

The *James Caird* is the 23-foot-long ship's boat which the explorer, Sir Ernest Shackleton, with five companions, sailed from Elephant Island, south of Cape Horn, to South Georgia,

The *James Caird* at Dulwich College

in 1916. This 800-mile voyage in an open boat, through the Southern Ocean in early winter, renowned among mariners for its fierce gales and enormous seas, ranks as one of the greatest feats of seamanship in the long history of seafaring.

Shackleton's boat is now preserved at Dulwich College, his old school in south London. But for the enthusiasm of some Norwegian whalers, who insisted on rescuing what remained of her from the ice-strewn beach where she had ended her voyage and shipping her on to England in 1919, she would not be here to remind us of that epic feat. Indeed, apart from the historic film and photographs taken by the expedition photographer Frank Hurley, and a Bible, a log, a sextant and a Primus stove, still preserved, the *James Caird* is almost all that remains of Shackleton's well-found expedition in the *Endurance*, which set out in 1914 to undertake the crossing of the Antarctic continent from the Weddell Sea to the Ross Sea, but met with disaster.

With four Antarctic expeditions to his credit, no man has left a more enduring mark nor stamped his personality more firmly on Antarctica than Shackleton. The map of the southern continent is littered with features that bear his name, from the Shackleton Range of mountains to a glacier, an ice fall, an inlet, a coast and many others. When Sir Vivian Fuchs led the Commonwealth Trans-Antarctic Expedition in 1955, he gave the name of 'Shackleton Base' to his starting point in honour of the man who had set out to cross the continent nearly half a century before.

Born near Dublin on 15 February 1874, but descended from a Yorkshire family, Ernest Henry Shackleton grew up in south London. Since he was determined to go to sea, his father, almost in desperation, arranged for him to leave his school, Dulwich College, early and at the age of sixteen, enter the hard world of square-rigged sailing ships. By good

Top: A square-rigger in a gale
Left: Shackleton as a boy

Left: Shackleton in cadet rig

fortune, Shackleton senior's cousin ran the Mission for Seamen in Liverpool, who saw to it that his nephew would be in the hands of a good captain. Bound apprentice to qualify as an officer, young Ernest rounded Cape Horn five times within two years and twice his ship was dismasted. He gained the reputation of being out of the usual run, a hard worker, a good mixer, a spellbinding storyteller and a lover of poetry, particularly the works of Browning, from which he could quote at length.

By 1898, at the early age of 24, he had gained his Master's 'ticket', which qualified him to command a British ship anywhere in the world. But the prospect of a relatively mundane life in ocean liners did not appeal to him. When the urge for adventure, fame and fortune coincided with opportunity, he grasped it eagerly. For the rest of his life, over a period of some twenty years, the frozen wastes of the Antarctic were to dominate his career and absorb all his abundant energy.

Thanks to a century of exploration by sea, land and air, the geography of Antarctica is now well documented. Two centuries ago no one even knew such a continent existed. Early explorers had sought new land in the south in the hope that, beyond the Tropic of Capricorn, a new El Dorado, to rival South America, waited in the South Pacific with vast riches in store for the nation fortunate enough to discover it.

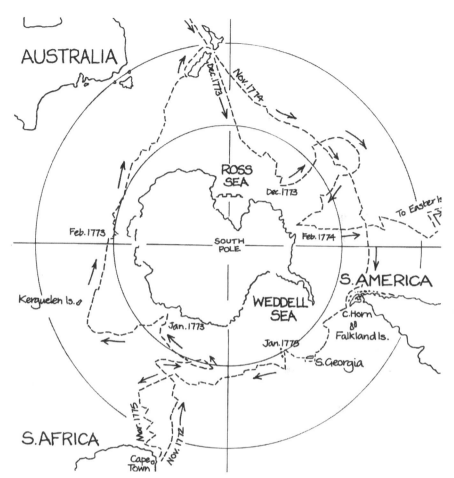

Track of Captain James Cook's expedition 1772–75

That a large land mass must exist in the Southern Hemisphere
was confirmed by Captain Cook, the great eighteenth-
century navigator. On his third voyage in 1774, Cook
reached the latitude of 71° 10' South, well beyond the
Antarctic Circle. In conditions of extreme cold, high seas and
gale-force winds, he was only halted by an impenetrable
barrier of pack ice. Cook reported that land almost certainly
existed beyond the ice barrier, because the ice of the
enormous bergs they encountered consisted of frozen fresh
water which could only come from land-based glaciers.

5

Above: Ross's ships *Erebus* and *Terror*
Left: Captain James Clark Ross RN

Nevertheless, any land could only be a wilderness of ice and snow, uninhabited and worthless.

Early in the nineteenth century a handful of explorers, including three Britons, Biscoe, Bransfield and Weddell, Bellingshausen, a Russian, and many others, ventured into the Southern Ocean. Accounts of their voyages brought a flood of seal hunters, and later, whalers, in their wake. None was able to penetrate the pack-ice barrier until Sir James Clark Ross – then Captain Ross RN – led an expedition to locate the South Magnetic Pole. With twenty years' experience in the Arctic, he was given carte blanche to equip his expedition. He sailed south with two vessels, *Erebus* and *Terror*, which had been specially strengthened and equipped for work in the ice.

In 1841 Ross approached the continent from the Pacific Ocean, forced a passage through the pack ice and broke through into clear water beyond. He gave his name to the Ross Sea but did not land on the continent, for he found a forbidding coastline of huge ice cliffs now known as the Ross Ice Shelf or Barrier. He had a view of mountains, 10,000 feet high, in the distance beyond. He also named Ross Island, which was distinguished by two huge volcanoes, towering straight out of the sea. He named them after his ships; Erebus rose to a height of over 12,000 feet and was still active, while Terror was only 1,500 feet lower. He penetrated beyond Ross Island and entered McMurdo Sound,[1] unwittingly discovering the nearest land approach to the South Pole.

Interest in the southern continent then lapsed until the end of the century, when the Sixth International Geographical Conference, held in London in 1895, issued a challenge to the nations to unravel the secrets of this vast unknown wilderness. Polar exploration until then had been concentrated on the Arctic, and the search for the North West Passage. In an atlas of that date, the first illustration showed the 'North Polar Chart', although a large area round the North Pole is marked 'unknown region'. There is no corresponding map of Antarctica. No one had ever set foot on it although its area was equal in size to the whole of North America. Protected by a barrier of ice which only Ross had pierced, surrounded in its turn by the Southern Ocean – the most storm-swept waters in the world – it was about to become the latest challenge to the world's explorers.

One of the first to respond was the Royal Geographical Society. Discussions had taken place on the possibilities of exploring in the Antarctic during the 1880s and early 1890s, and in 1893 plans began to take shape under its president, Sir Clements Markham. Shortly afterwards the formation of the National Antarctic Expedition was announced. The Royal Society was invited to take part because of the magnitude of the task, but soon Sir Clements became concerned that he might lose control of his pet scheme. Arguments between the two Societies delayed the plans and in 1897 a Belgian expedition, led by de Gerlache in the *Belgica*, stole a march on the British. A member of the crew was a Norwegian, by the name of Roald Amundsen. This was

Shackleton, 3rd Officer, Union
Castle Line

Sub-Lieutenant Shackleton RNR

followed by a private British venture sponsored by Newnes, a newspaper magnate, with a party made up of many nationalities led by Borchgrevink, a Norwegian, in 1898.

The National Antarctic Expedition eventually sailed from England in August 1901, with Lieutenant, later Captain Robert Falcon Scott RN in command, while Ernest Shackleton was required to become a sub-lieutenant (RNR) in order to serve as Third Officer, for Markham intended that the expedition should be a Royal Navy one. A ship of timber construction, designed for work among the ice floes, was built in Dundee and named *Discovery*. They were closely followed by Scottish, German and French expeditions.

The ship and her company were inspected by King Edward VII and Queen Alexandra at Cowes, where the Royal Yacht was attending the annual regatta in the Solent. They sailed via New Zealand, reached the Ross Sea ice barrier on New Year's Day, breaking through it to land at McMurdo Sound, setting up a shore base in February 1902 and wintering there until October.

Discovery passes the Royal Yacht at Cowes, 1901, a painting by Gerald M. Burn at Dulwich College

Shackleton, third from left, and Scott, centre in frock coat, with *Discovery* colleagues

Shackleton, Scott and Wilson, 1902

On 2 November a party consisting of Scott, Shackleton and Wilson set off south into the unknown, on the first attempt to reach the South Pole. Through inexperience, incorrect diet, unsuitable clothing and equipment and their inability to manage sledge-hauling with dog teams, they had to turn back, less than halfway to their goal. The expedition remained for a second winter, but Scott sent Shackleton home on the relief ship, *Morning*, much to the latter's dismay.

Louis Bernacchi, the only member of the expedition who already had experience in the Antarctic, wrote of him:

> Just as he had been in his former ships, Shackleton was the life and soul of *Discovery*. His mind was alert, his good humour inexhaustible. Besides being in charge of the holds and the stores, he carried out his ordinary duties as an executive officer. He was a fine self-reliant seaman, fearless and dominant, with a stern regard for detail and discipline. He permitted no liberties from those under his command, and could be brutally truculent if such occasion arose. But he was singularly sympathetic, and understanding.[2]

In fact, the cause of their sickness was scurvy, from which all three had suffered. Shackleton recovered in a matter of hours – faster than the others – on a diet of fresh seal meat. He saw to it that he never suffered from scurvy again.

In 1907 Shackleton, who disliked being under the control of the men who ran the learned societies, organised his own expedition, depending on private sponsorship to finance his plans. He sailed south in August, with his chosen party, his principal aim being to reach the South Pole. As he passed through the English Channel in his ship *Nimrod*, he and his party were inspected at Cowes by the King, Queen Alexandra and other members of the Royal family. At the last moment the King produced, out of his frock coat pocket, the medal

King Edward VII visits
Nimrod at Cowes

of the Royal Victorian Order and pinned it on Shackleton's breast.

After leaving New Zealand they survived a very rough voyage to the Ross Sea, experiencing a week-long hurricane and very high seas, much of it with *Nimrod* under tow by the steamship *Koonya* to save coal for use at their future base. The tow was a triumph of seamanship on the part of Captain Evans in the *Koonya*. They built a hut a few miles north of *Discovery*'s mooring and sent *Nimrod* back to New Zealand for the winter.

The expedition had its first success when a party of six climbed the 12,000-foot-high volcano Mount Erebus on Ross Island. It had been active when Ross discovered it but on this occasion it was dormant so that the party was able, in safety, to inspect the inside of the crater.

Nimrod in a gale under tow by *Koonya*, a painting by George Marston, the expedition artist

Early in October, Edgworth David, Douglas Mawson and Alastair Mackay set off for the South Magnetic Pole, Shackleton's secondary objective, known to be in South Victoria Land. They eventually located it after a very difficult and arduous journey. During their return, conditions were even worse, and after four months of arduous travel, they were lucky to survive.

On 9 October 1908, a four-man party comprising Shackleton, Wild, Adams and Marshall started on their great adventure. The round journey to the Pole was some 1,700 miles, the major part of the route unexplored. They made good going across the Ross Ice Shelf until they came to the great range of mountains that lay obliquely across their path. They found a route through this barrier up a vast glacier,

The Beardmore Glacier

Shackleton in polar rig

which Shackleton named the Beardmore Glacier after his main sponsor. At 150 miles long, it proved to be the key to his problem for it led them steadily upwards through dangerous icefalls and crevasse-riven terrain to the plateau, 11,000 feet high, where their goal lay.

The existence of this feature was quite unexpected and they were unaware that ice, 7,500 feet thick, overlaid the rock beneath them. Finally they reached 88° 23' South, only 97 miles short of the South Pole, a point since known as the 'Furthest South' – at that time the nearest to either Pole reached by man. There Shackleton took the momentous decision, almost in sight of his goal, to turn back. He knew that *Nimrod* had to sail for New Zealand at the end of March, to avoid being frozen in for the winter. He had laid down the last date for her departure. Time

'Furthest South' only 97 miles from the South Pole, 1909

and food supply dictated retreat, in order to reach base by that deadline. Their return journey became a race for survival, which, by determination and almost superhuman efforts, they won by a hair's breadth. Shackleton's final effort was described by Wordie, one of the scientists on the *Endurance* expedition:

> The story of their return march is one of magnificent courage and endurance. Their daily average was eighteen miles on three-quarter rations (man-pulling). And at the end of it all, Shackleton performed the astonishing feat of going back with the relief party for two members who had broken down. By doing this he covered 100 miles without rest on top of a 1,700 mile journey.[3]

Later, some criticised Shackleton for turning back so near his goal, but he saw no point in risking the lives of his

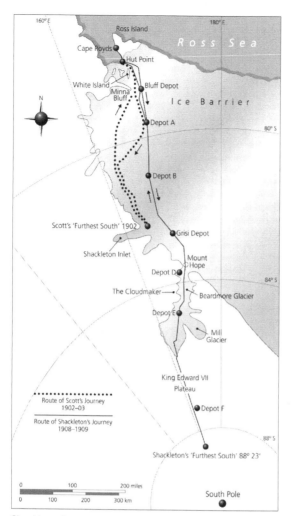

Shackleton's route towards the South Pole

companions, for which, as their leader, he was responsible, let alone his own. Nansen, the great Norwegian explorer, had made a similar decision when the North Pole was almost within his reach, twelve years before. In both cases, the decision to turn back took very great courage. Shackleton remarked to his wife later: 'I thought you would prefer a live donkey to a dead lion.' News of their exploits was cabled home when they reached New Zealand and, by the time he returned to London in June 1909, Shackleton had become a national hero.

The Arrol-Johnston car on skis during the *Nimrod* expedition

A safe return. Wild, Shackleton, Marshall and Adams

Shackleton dined by
the Alleyn Club

Shackleton returns to Dulwich, 1909

It must be remembered that this was a time of great
international rivalry. The greatest empire in history which
covered one quarter of the globe was in its golden age,
celebrated by jingoism, in Kipling's stirring verses and in
Elgar's *Land of Hope and Glory*. Shackleton was fêted
everywhere and invited to stay at Balmoral, the royal retreat
in the highlands of Scotland, to describe his adventures, to
Berlin by the Kaiser, to St Petersburg by the Tsar and Tsarina
and to Christiania – now Oslo – by the Norwegians. The
generous and emotional welcome extended by Nansen and
Amundsen, acknowledged as the greatest explorers of the

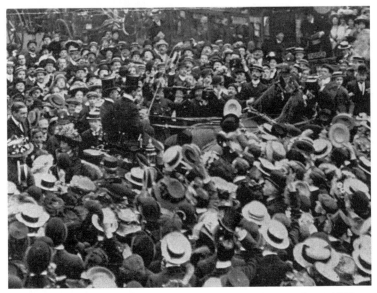

Above: Shackleton is welcomed home in London at Charing Cross, 1909
Below: Shackleton wears his decorations

day, was appreciated by Shackleton above all else, for they understood, from their personal experience, what he had endured and what he had achieved. Honours were showered on him throughout Europe and America and he was knighted by the King.

When the fame of his 'Furthest South' achievements had faded somewhat, a newspaper reported that, contrary to the general assumption that fame and fortune were his, this national hero, Shackleton, was broke and deeply in debt. Popular pressure on the government eventually extracted a grant of £20,000 to help him settle his affairs. It appears that Lady Shackleton had dropped a quiet hint to the wife of a newspaper proprietor.

2

THE LAST
GREAT ANTARCTIC
ADVENTURE

*I*n 1913 Shackleton had a new ambition. The South
Pole had fallen to Amundsen in 1911 and to the ill-
fated Scott a month later. He now saw the crossing of
the Antarctic continent from the Weddell Sea to the Ross Sea
via the South Pole as 'the last great Antarctic adventure'.
Again, he organised his own expedition – he avoided

Amundsen reaches the South Pole, 1911   Amundsen

Fram, which Amundsen borrowed from Nansen in 1910

Endurance at London docks

dependence on officialdom and learned institutions. He planned to sail in one ship with his main party to South Georgia and then through the Weddell Sea to Vahsel Bay, and the Filchner Ice Shelf, where he believed that a landing would be possible. Meanwhile, a second ship would take another party to McMurdo Sound on the Ross Sea, to lay supply depots between the old base there and the bottom of the Beardmore Glacier, to await his arrival, after a sledge journey of nearly 1,000 miles across the continent.[4] The terrain from Vahsel Bay to the Pole was unexplored. Shackleton, of course, knew from his own experience that it would entail a climb of 11,000 feet through virgin mountain ranges. He knew well the extremes of weather that he would have to face and the treacherous surfaces on the glaciers that awaited him.

Shackleton began to plan in the middle of 1913 but did not make an official announcement until the following January. By this time he had been given enough promises of funds to encourage him to proceed. Small offers of money came from many parts of the world and thousands of requests came to join the expedition. The British government contributed £10,000 and substantial help came from wealthy individuals including Dudley Docker, Miss Janet Stancomb Wills and Mrs Elizabeth Dawson Lambton. The Public

Sir James Caird, Shackleton's principal sponsor

Schools of England and Scotland subscribed specifically for purchasing dog teams. He bought two ships, one in Norway, which he renamed *Endurance*, and a second, the *Aurora*, in Tasmania. But by the summer of 1914, funds were still short and Shackleton found himself with many uncertain promises and not enough hard cash. It was a very worrying time for him, because, apart from money problems, the threat of war in Europe developed midway through 1914, which created uncertainty on the part of possible sponsors.

Then, out of the blue, in the middle of June, an invitation to visit him in Dundee came from a Sir James Key Caird. Caird was a wealthy jute manufacturer, a widower, whose only child had died. He was a friend of Winston Churchill, then the sitting Member of Parliament for Dundee, and a philanthropist who had given Dundee £100,000 to build a city hall, among many other benefactions. He gave no reason for the invitation but apparently he had taken a liking to this enthusiastic explorer and had learned of his predicament.

Shackleton at once hurried north, met the austere Scot who listened intently to his plans and then asked quietly about his finances. Shackleton explained the pledges and guarantees, which he had been required to give to various sponsors. According to H. R. Mill, Shackleton's friend and biographer, Caird then said: 'Do you think, Sir Ernest, that these gentlemen would release you from that obligation if you were to tell them there was a man in Scotland who would find the remaining £24,000 on that condition?' Shackleton nearly fell off his chair. Here was an end to his financial anxieties and he assured Sir James that he could do what he asked. Within a week the promised cheque arrived with a letter to say that it was a gift without any conditions. With his sailing date only five weeks away, it was a close-run thing. Today, that sum would be worth over three-quarters of a million pounds sterling.

In the meantime Shackleton had chosen the men to accompany him. Frank Wild, a companion from the 1901–02 expedition and his staunchest supporter during the 'Furthest South' expedition in 1907–09, was to be second in command; Frank Worsley, from New Zealand and a first-rate navigator, was appointed Master, in command of *Endurance*. Worsley had joined the expedition quite by chance. He had dreamed, one night, of icebergs in Burlington Street, near Piccadilly, had walked down that street next morning, had seen the expedition's sign outside its office door, walked in and, after a few minutes conversation with Shackleton, was taken on. That was the way the explorer chose his men – he made up his mind quickly and said 'yes' or 'no'. Some had no idea why they were selected. In Shackleton's team each man had to be prepared to do any job he was asked to do and even scientists could find

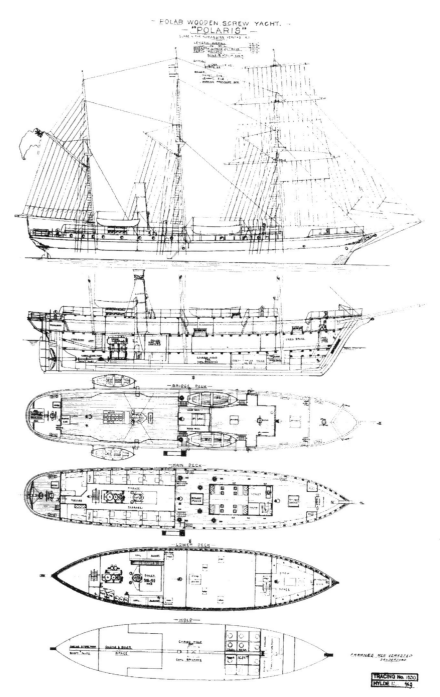

A drawing of *Endurance* from the archives of the builders, Framnaes Mek. Verksted of Sandefjord, Norway. Originally *Polaris*, Shackleton renamed her after his family motto 'By endurance we conquer'.

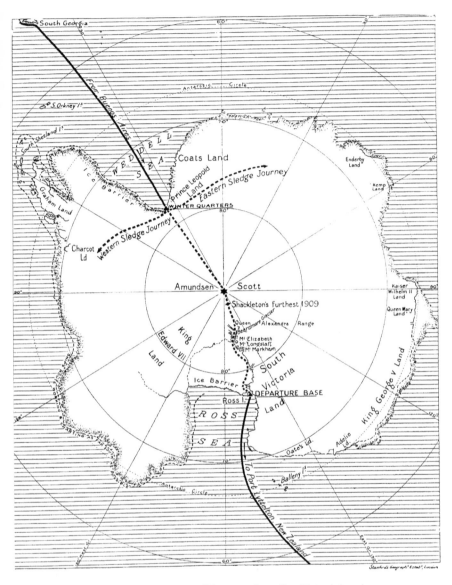

'The last great Antarctic adventure.' The map from Shackleton's brochure announcing his Imperial Trans-Antarctic Expedition shows how little was known of Antarctica in 1914.

Shackleton shows Queen Alexandra around his ship

themselves scrubbing the deck. Life on board was to be classless and everyone was expected to 'muck in'.

The *Endurance* was a new ship, specially designed and built at Sandefjord in Norway for work in the ice. Shackleton bought her with two ship's boats and, in June, had her sailed over to London and berthed for loading in Millwall dock, in London's Isle of Dogs. In July, Worsley took delivery of a third ship's boat, built, according to his book *Endurance*,[5] to his own specifications, in a boatyard on the Thames, nearby. She was a little larger than the two Norwegian boats.

During July, there were many visitors to the ship, among them Queen Alexandra, by then a dowager, who brought her sister, Maria Feodorovna, the Dowager Empress of Russia. Shackleton had been rather a favourite of Queen Alexandra's

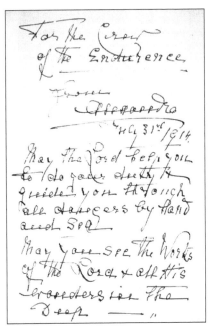

Queen Alexandra (left), with her sister, Maria Feodorovna, Dowager Empress of Russia, Lady Shackleton and her son, Eddie, the future Lord Shackleton (right)

The flyleaf from Queen Alexandra's Bible

Sir Ernest and Lady Shackleton visit *Endurance*

ever since they met on *Discovery*, thirteen years before. She presented the ship with a Bible, inscribing a farewell message on the flyleaf. At the same time his wife, Emily, brought their younger son, Edward, who later became Lord Shackleton.

Towards the end of July the threat of war in Europe had become a serious possibility. At the beginning of August 1914, *Endurance* sailed from Millwall dock, reaching Margate, at the mouth of the Thames, on 3 August, to find that mobilisation was under way. Two members of the ship's company had already left to join their regiments. All his plans appeared to be on the point of collapse. With the consent of his men, Shackleton offered to turn *Endurance* and her crew over to the Admiralty. The offer was declined. In a typically laconic gesture the First Lord of the Admiralty, Winston Churchill, telegraphed the one-word response 'Proceed'. War was declared on 4 August, although the general belief was that it would be over by Christmas. The next day the King sent for Shackleton, to wish him luck, and on 8 August, *Endurance* sailed from Plymouth for Madeira, Buenos Aires and South Georgia. They spent a month there getting to know the Norwegian station managers and the conditions in the Southern Ocean, and learning all they could about the task ahead.

On 5 December the *Endurance* sailed south from South Georgia into the Weddell Sea, trying to skirt the pack ice which the whalers at Grytviken had reported to be much further north than usual for an Antarctic summer. It was a bad outlook. Ahead was a voyage of 1,000 miles to the coast of Antarctica, which had been surveyed partially by the Scots explorer W. S. Bruce and named Coats Land in 1902. In fact, Bruce had intended to attempt the trans-Antarctic crossing himself in 1911, but when he could not raise the necessary finance, he offered the idea to Shackleton.

Following a course to the south-east *Endurance* made reasonable progress for some 400 miles, but then had to

The crew of *Endurance*

thread her way through loose ice until she came up against the pack ice. This comprised large areas of frozen sea with broken pieces of ice of all sizes, including huge icebergs and flat pancake ice all jumbled up together. These ice islands were separated by leads of open water through which a ship could sail. Inevitably, progress in these conditions was slow, as *Endurance* skirted the edges of the ice, weaving this way and that to find a safe passage. After a month, when several days were spent unable to proceed, they managed to break free into open water. On 10 January 1915, after five weeks at sea, land was sighted which, from Bruce's description, was recognised as Coats Land.

They were able to sail in a south-westerly direction towards Vahsel Bay, with a coastline of high ice cliffs and

To Captain Bernsten in remembrance of a pleasant day, with kindest regards E H Shackleton Jan 1914

Shackleton welcomes Norwegian whalers to *Endurance*. Shackleton at left, Mr Sørlle at right, Worsley, second from right

large crevasse-riven glaciers in view. This new land they named 'Caird Coast', in honour of their main sponsor but on 19 January the pack closed round *Endurance* and, in spite of their best efforts to free her, she remained held fast. Then she began to drift with the pack and on 22 January reached their furthest position south. For the next nine months, from January to October 1915, she drifted slowly northwards for 1,000 miles, still held fast in the pack ice, which moved clockwise in a wide circular direction within the Weddell Sea. In March the Antarctic winter set in and, for nearly three months, from the end of May until the end of August, the sun never rose above the horizon. The temperature dropped

Endurance at Leith Harbour, South Georgia

Endurance in the pack ice

Caird Coast

Endurance under sail

The threat to *Endurance*

Ice blocks threaten *Endurance*

Endurance – the memorable view

Endurance lit up – Hurley's famous night view

to 30, 40 and 50 degrees below zero and blizzards driving at 50 miles per hour were frequent, lasting sometimes for days. Yet, despite these appalling conditions and the uncertain outlook, morale remained remarkably high.

Meanwhile, the tremendous pressures and continuous movement contorted the ice floes and icebergs, some over 100 feet high, which surrounded *Endurance*. Huge blocks

Endurance breaking up

The end of *Endurance*

weighing many tons were lifted into the air and tossed aside as others rose beneath them. Plans were made to move dogs, stores, sledges, equipment and boats at a moment's notice. On 27 October, huge pressures began to crush her timbers and the ship was abandoned, being too dangerous to enter. From then on the expedition lived in tents, naming their new home 'Ocean Camp'. On 21 November, *Endurance* finally broke up and sank. The loss of their ship was a traumatic experience for everyone.

3

PREPARING THE
JAMES CAIRD

*S*hackleton, who was never found wanting in such matters, had realised long before that their survival would depend on their three lifeboats. While timber was available, he instructed McNeish, the ship's carpenter, to build up the sides of the largest of the three, to increase her carrying capacity and improve her seaworthiness. This proved to be a far-sighted decision with immeasurable consequences later on. While timber was still available and working conditions on the ice were not too severe, McNeish added two more strakes (the planking on the sides of the boat, running lengthwise), raised the thwarts (the transverse wooden planks used as seats) and finally, according to Worsley's diary (see below), added half-decks fore and aft – he termed them 'whale-backs' – to keep out seas and provide some shelter for stores stowed beneath. His diary goes on to give an account of what was done:

21 Nov. 1915
The carpenter and his assistants work all day to complete the whaler. The work on her must not be interrupted for fear that the floes might break up before she is quite ready to take the water.

22 Nov. 1915

Carpenter finishes building topsides, forward and after whalebacks on whaler and fits pump, made by Hurley, into her. All that now remains is to calk [i.e. caulk] her topsides. She could now, at a pinch, carry 29 men. She can carry 6½ tons measurement or 3½ tons deadweight besides her gear. [Incidentally, Hurley, the expedition photographer, made the pump 'from the Flinders bar casing of the ship's compass', Worsley explains later.]

23 Nov. 1915

Carpenter calking [*sic*] topsides of whaler with cotton threadwick. We have not been able to secure pitch, putty or ship's paints, but Marston's oil colours come in very handy for covering and filling up the seams, possibly the first time that artist's colours have been used for 'paying' the seams of a ship's boat. Rickenson (the chief engineer) makes a rudder for the whaler. [Marston was the expedition artist.]

24 Nov. 1915

Carpenter finishes off the whaler and starts to calk the 2nd cutter [the *Stancomb Wills*].

25 Nov. 1915

Cut down the second cutter's lugsail into a mizen for the whaler, for which the carpr. fits her with a small mizzen mast, cut down from second cutter's mast. The whaler is already fitted with a standing lug and jib, the first whaler [meaning cutter?] with a dipping lug.

Shackleton called the crew together on 26 November, to tell them that the three boats[6] were their only hope of survival and announced a christening ceremony. The two Norwegian-built boats were named the *Dudley Docker* and the

Stancomb Wills, after two of the expedition's main benefactors. The largest of the three – the whaler on which the carpenter had worked, was named the *James Caird*, after the man who had made the expedition possible with his unexpected and dramatic last-minute gift. Apparently this ceremony made little impression on Worsley for he merely records in his diary: 'Sir Ernest names the boats as follows: Whaler *James Caird*, 1st Cutter *Dudley Docker*, 2nd Cutter *Stancomb Wills*.' On 27 November, he lists the crew of the *James Caird*: 'Sir Ernest Shackleton, F. Wild, Vincent, McCarty [*sic*], Hurley, carpenter [i.e. McNeish], James Wordie, Hussey, Clark, Green.'

Two weeks later the *James Caird* was put through a buoyancy test in a lead or channel, which had opened up between two ice floes. It was presumably her first trial in the water since the expedition left South Georgia. Worsley's diary entry describes it:

8 Dec. 1915
In the morning we haul the *James Caird* 250 yards and launch her into the water from her sledge in 6½ minutes, taking it easily. Previously we had cut an incline down to the water, thro. the edge of the floe, appears a little crank when empty, but quite stable when loaded with six sledge loads of stores and 11 men who total at 160 lbs each with clothes. With this load she has 2 ft 2 ins freeboard, and would probably settle a couple of inches deeper. After marking and measuring her we pulled her clear out of water. From start of unloading till she was clear up on the floe = 5½ minutes.

They repeated this exercise until their drill was satisfactory, experimenting with a variety of tackles and methods of unloading. It was to be vital in the days ahead to prevent the

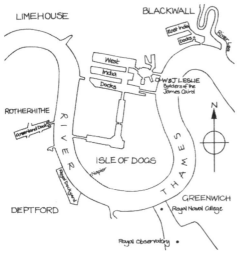

A part of the River Thames in 1910 shows the boatyard of W. & J. Leslie where the *James Caird* was built

boats from being caught in a lead and crushed between two floes as they crashed together.

The *James Caird* was originally Frank Worsley's 'baby'. It was he who had her built, to his own specifications, by W. & J. Leslie, a boat builder at Coldharbour, Poplar, near the northern entrance to the West India docks downstream from the Tower of London on the north bank of the Thames, where a big loop almost encircles the Isle of Dogs (modern-day Canary Wharf). The River Thames hereabouts had, for generations, been renowned for ship and boat building. There had been a Royal Dockyard at Deptford, on the south shore, at the time of Henry VIII, flourishing during the seventeenth century, when Pepys was at the Navy Office, and then through the eighteenth and nineteenth centuries. In the 1850s, Brunel's huge *Great Eastern* was built at the Napier Yard, Millwall, in the Isle of Dogs, across the river from Deptford. At that time, the concentration of smaller yards in Rotherhithe, Deptford, Millwall, Blackwall and Woolwich produced one quarter of all the ships' lifeboats built in the United Kingdom, supplying the needs of the yards that built the big ships.

In one of his accounts of the *Endurance* expedition, Worsley gives his specifications for the *James Caird*:

She was double-ended and clinker-built[7] to my orders in July 1914. ... The planking was Baltic pine, keel and timbers American elm, stem- and sternpost English oak. She was more lightly built than is required by the Board of Trade. This made her springy and buoyant.

The *James Caird* ... was 22 feet 6 inches long[8] with a 6 foot beam. [He does not give the depth, as built]. I had worked out the maximum load which she could safely carry as 3½ tons.

The *Dudley Docker* was 22 feet long, 6 feet wide and 3 feet deep with a safe load of 1½ tons, while the *Stancomb Wills* he gives as 20 feet 8 inches long by 5 feet 6 inches in the beam, 2 feet 3½ inches deep 'from inside of her keel to the top of her gunwale'. Referring to the *Caird* again, he adds: 'She had been raised until her depth was 3 feet 7 inches.'

Later he wrote: 'The carpenter had built her 15 inches higher', so presumably the built depth was 2 feet 4 inches, although in his diary, he makes this 1 inch lower, when calculating the boat's carrying capacity.

At one stage McNeish offered to build a cutter from the timbers of the *Endurance*, in which, he maintained, they could return to civilisation when the ice broke up. The 'Boss' – everyone addressed Shackleton as 'Boss' – turned down the idea as impractical. It has been suggested that Shackleton's real reason was that he always had a small boat journey at the back of his mind. He certainly knew of the feat of Carl Larsen, whose ship *Antarctic* had been crushed in the ice twelve years before near Paulet Island and foundered. After six months in a rock hut on the island Larsen, with three companions, had then rowed a ship's lifeboat for 100 miles to Snow Hill Island, near the tip of Graham Land, where Nordenskjöld, the expedition leader, had wintered. It was always clear to Shackleton, once he had lost his ship, that his small boats were his only hope of survival.

Ocean Camp

Harry McNeish, the ship's carpenter, was a very important member of the expedition. A Scot from Dundee, he was a big, strong man, although in his forties and the oldest member of the crew. In the days of wooden sailing ships, a carpenter in the Navy was a Warrant Officer and so enjoyed a special status. In a large vessel he rated a cabin of his own and was known as an 'idler', who was not required to stand watches. The same held good in the Merchant Service. They were skilled craftsmen, responsible for the hull, masts and spars. After a battle, or a dismasting, their skills were vital. This status and his native independence of outlook explain, to some extent, what happened not long after the celebrations for Christmas in 1915.

Life on the ice in Ocean Camp, as they called it, could be very miserable and Shackleton was concerned to keep everyone as busy as possible. He pressed forward their efforts to reach land, partly to maintain morale, so it was decided to haul the boats over the ice. Shackleton and Wild would survey a route through the wilderness of hummocks, then a path had to be levelled and the ice chopped back on either side, to prevent damage to the hulls. The boats were placed onto sledges and dragged by dog teams or man-hauled along the prepared track. It was back-breaking work, made worse when the softness of the snow – it was the austral midsummer – allowed the men to sink in up to their knees. In the first eight-hour stint they moved the *James Caird* a mere mile and a quarter.

They soon changed to night-hauling, because the surface froze into a crust sufficiently hard to support them and there was daylight for twenty-four hours. After several nights of hauling the *James Caird* and the *Dudley Docker*, McNeish rebelled and refused to pull. He was suffering from piles and the effort was agonising. He pointed out that, after their ship had sunk, a crew was no longer bound by their contract. Shackleton had to act fast to avoid a possible mutiny. A barrack-room lawyer was the last thing he needed. He gathered everyone round him and read out the terms of their

contract; he announced that he was, in fact, the Master of *Endurance*, and that they would all receive full pay until they got home. It was all a bit specious but it worked and McNeish, after a 'heart to heart' with the Boss, went back to work. Shackleton never forgave him for his lapse in loyalty. After

McNeish

Shackleton and Wild survey a route

seven days they gave up hauling, exhausted. They had gained no more than 7½ miles in a direct line.

With the coming of summer, leads had begun to appear in the ice floes and as January 1916 advanced, what had appeared to be a continuous sea of ice became vast floating ice islands. These separated and came together again with alarming violence, the position of Ocean Camp changing continually with the drifting of the floes. Meanwhile, Shackleton was growing concerned about the food supply. The hunt for penguins and seals was intensified to supplement, particularly, the supply of seals, because their blubber was essential for heating the cooking stove. Twice Shackleton sent Macklin and Hurley back to their old camp to recover supplies they had left behind. Then on 2 February, when their new camp had drifted to within 5 miles of Ocean Camp he sent Wild, with a team of eighteen men, to bring back as much food and clothing and as many books as possible. They also brought the third boat, the *Stancomb*

Shackleton in Patience Camp

Wills, and settled down to wait in 'Patience Camp', as they had christened their new quarters.

During the next two months, lack of action, shortage of food and the continued uncertainty about their future made existence on the ice more difficult than ever. On two occasions, blizzards raged for five and six days keeping them tent-bound except for the bare essentials. On one nerve-racking day large bergs were watched in alarm as they charged through the pack, heading straight for Patience Camp, leaving chaos behind them. At the last moment they changed direction and the camp was spared, otherwise nothing could have saved them.

Their likely destination, when the pack broke up and they had to take to their boats, provided an endless guessing game. Could they reach Paulet Island? They knew there was food in a hut there, because Shackleton had helped assemble supplies in 1903 for the relief ship sent to rescue the Nordenskjöld expedition. The alternatives appeared to be Clarence Island or Elephant Island in the South Shetlands group.

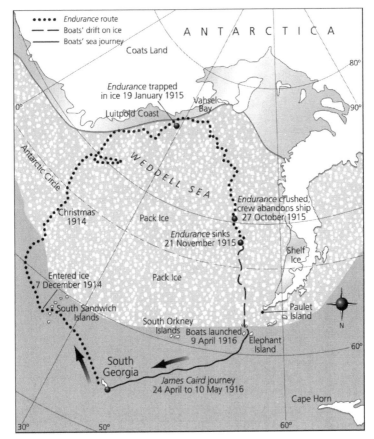

The track of *Endurance*

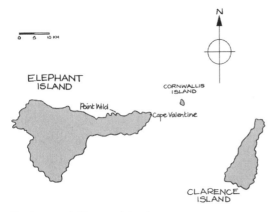

Elephant and Clarence Islands

Another scene at Ocean Camp

All this time, the Boss seemed to radiate an atmosphere of quiet confidence that all would be well in the end. There is no doubt this was the essential element in maintaining the general morale. In spite of the hardship and appalling conditions of life on the ice floes, his men had an unshakeable faith that he would see them through, although the 'how' or the 'when' was in the lap of the gods. His men depended on him for everything, and he had the uncanny ability always to be on the spot when he was needed. As March gave way to April, some sensed that he had become more taciturn and moody – hardly surprising in a man of action, who had to bottle up his natural impatience while he waited for the right opportunity to take to the boats. In spite of his outward signs of confidence, his diary notes betray his anxieties.

In the meantime their floe had swept them north of the Antarctic Circle. Shortage of food then made it necessary to shoot the remaining dogs, a sad occasion, for they had been their faithful companions for months past, regarded more as pets than working dogs. By then the party had spent ten months in the ice, first living in the ship and then in Ocean Camp, followed by four months more in Patience Camp. With the floes breaking up and getting smaller, even threatening to break under their camp, Shackleton decided it was time to leave. On 9 April they prepared to launch the three boats and take their chance.

In his book *Endurance*, Worsley tells how he discussed with Shackleton their best plan of action when the possibility arose of sailing to Joinville or Paulet Islands on the Antarctic peninsula. He writes:

> I said, of course you are right ... Nordenskjöld had only 25 miles to go. We should have 60. It would be a terrible thing if something happened to the expedition now, after you've brought us nearly 2,000 miles north in safety since the ship was first beset.
>
> Shackleton nodded and said: 'I can't risk the danger of crossing ice that will be opening and closing rapidly under the influence of the tides and currents, between us and the land. The boats might get crushed. We might get separated. Many things could happen. But if we keep on as we are for another hundred miles or so, we are bound to drift to open water, and then we can make for the nearest whaling station.'

4

THE *JAMES CAIRD*
LEADS THE WAY

Shackleton led in the *James Caird* followed by Worsley in the *Dudley Docker* with Hudson in command of the *Stancomb Wills*. In the *Caird* were Wild, Wordie, Hurley, Hussey, Clark, James, McNeish, McCarthy, Green and Vincent.[9] Outside the pack ice they faced the gales and violent seas for which these latitudes are renowned. The ice floes had, by then, drifted beyond the northern tip of Graham Land and it was no longer possible to reach the islands which the whale-catchers were known to visit. Their goal had to be Elephant Island or Clarence Island almost 500 miles south of Cape Horn.

As Shackleton wrote: 'Clarence Island was still more than sixty miles away, but it had to our eyes something of the appearance of home, since we expected to find there our first solid footing after all the long months of drifting on the unstable ice ... Our drifting home had no rudder to guide it, no sail to give it speed. We were dependent on the caprice of wind and current; we went where those irresponsible forces listed. The longing to feel solid earth under our feet filled our hearts.'

Worsley in the *Dudley Docker* gives a graphic account of the journey:

Apr 9, Sunday, 1916.
Position 61° 56'S, 53° 56'W. Moderate south-west to south-east breezes, overcast stratus and cumulo-stratus. It is to be hoped the south-east breeze will hold and so save us from drifting east of Clarence. [Clarence lay 12 miles east of Elephant Island.] If we drive past these islands, out to the open sea, it would have meant the end for 28 men crowded in small boats.

At 7 a.m. lanes of water and leads were seen on the western horizon, with loose ice but not yet workable for boats, as a long swell running from northwest was bumping the floes together. In any case we could not have forced the boats through the brash ice between the floes. We packed everything ready for launching and struck the tents.

1 p.m. The pack at last opened enough to launch the boats, taking sledging stores, tents, seal blubber for fuel and food. By 1.30 we had launched, loaded and pulled clear into an area of partially open water. Shackleton had one sledge across the stern of the *James Caird* and the *Dudley Docker* towed another. We found it impossible to manoeuvre through heavy ice with such hindrances and were forced to abandon the sledges.

2 p.m. Having made one mile on our way we were nearly caught by a heavy rush of pack-ice that drove towards us at three miles an hour. Two walls were converging, as well as overtaking us, with a wave of foaming water in front. We only just managed by pulling our damndest for an hour to save ourselves and the boats from being nipped and crushed. It was a hot hour in spite of the freezing temperature. Sir Ernest had cut our meals down to seal meat and blubber only, with seven ounces of

They hauled up the boats for the night. A painting by George Marston

dried milk per day for the party.

Six-fifteen. Getting dark. Have rowed seven miles northwest. Forced to stop and camp owing to danger in the darkness of the boats getting crushed by the crowding floes. Just then a long floe barred our course, so we hauled up on to it. There was the added inducement of plenty of food – a crabeater seal was there before us. It was soon killed and cut up. As we hauled up the boats, secured them and the stores and pitched the tents, Green, aided by How, cooked the best cuts.

In his book *South*,[10] Shackleton gives an account – less graphic than Worsley's – of their trials and tribulations. The ice floes kept splitting. On one occasion their floe split right

The three boats in a lead, the *James Caird* at right. A painting by George Marston

The three boats make progress. A painting by George Marston

There was no sleep that night. A painting by George Marston

underneath the spot where his sleeping bag had moulded a depression in the ice, and on the next night it split under one of the tents occupied by the men. Shackleton, who always appeared to be on hand in an emergency, saw a shape in the water and, with a mighty heave, pulled a man, still in his sleeping bag, right out of the water, just before two floes crashed together. In the darkness, he himself became separated from the others, marooned on a small floe, as they shifted their boats and gear to a larger one. Wild had to launch a boat to rescue him. Shackleton goes on: 'We were now on a piece of flat ice about 200 ft. long and 100 ft. wide. There was no more sleep for us that night. The killers were blowing in the lanes around and we waited for daylight and watched for signs of another crack in the ice.'

Killer whales lurked in the leads

Worsley's account of this incident is almost jocular: 'No more sleep. Killers were blowing all round. All hands kept warm by tramping the floe and huddling round the blazing fire of seal blubber till dawn. Every two hours we cooked more seal meat and had another meal. To prevent boredom Mickey told us how to make eleven varieties of cocktail with scandalous names for each ... We amused ourselves so well till dawn that, in spite of 25° of frost, we almost imagined we were on a picnic.'

Next morning the boats set sail again and found a stretch of open water. Shackleton takes up the story: 'A strong easterly breeze was blowing but the fringe of pack lying outside protected us from the full force of the swell ... Soon after noon we swung round the end of the pack and laid a course to the westward, the *James Caird* still in the lead. Immediately our deeply-laden boats began to make heavy weather. They shipped sprays which, freezing as they fell, covered men and gear with ice, and soon it was clear that we could not safely proceed. I put the *James Caird* round and ran for the shelter of the pack again, the other boats following.'

The reeling berg. A painting by George Marston

A detail of the reeling berg shows the *James Caird* with mast. A painting by George Marston

There they hauled up the boats for the night and cooked a meal. The next day the floes had closed up and there was no open water visible even from the top of their small berg. They had to wait until late in the morning before conditions improved. Shackleton wrote: 'Slowly the open water came nearer and at noon it had almost reached us ... We rushed our boats over the edge of the reeling berg and swung them clear of the ice-foot as it rose beneath them. The *James Caird* was nearly capsized by a blow from below as the berg rolled away. We flung gear and stores into the boat and within a few minutes were away. The *James Caird* and the *Dudley Docker* had good sails and with a favourable breeze could make progress along the lane, with rolling fields of ice on either side.'

Progress was disappointing, as Worsley explains: 'So far this boat escape had been a "rake's progress". We had rowed, we had sailed. Shackleton and I had taken turns in towing the smallest boat. We had been hindered by pack-ice, head winds, currents and heavy swells. Now, after three days of toil and exposure, without sleep, we were 40 miles further from Elephant Island. In spite of all, the men inspired by Shackleton were magnificent. Their courage and humour came to the front when most needed. It was well that they had been toughened and tempered to hardness for this ordeal, by the progressively severer conditions which we had undergone since leaving civilisation.'

On the fourth day they had a fair wind and an open sea at last. Worsley continues: 'Sailing on at a fair rate, we came into an area of loose pack interspersed with many lumps. Taking turns we leaned over the bows, poling the lumps away with indifferent success. Many were too large to be moved quickly enough. The *Caird* struck one that holed her above the waterline. Soon after we saw a piece of sealskin protruding through the hole to keep the water out. After that we reefed sails to avoid more damage to the boats ... We made good headway, but had to take a second reef in the sails, as the boats were shipping much water and steering badly in the rising wind and sea.'

Later they landed for the night: 'Our floeberg was 90 feet long and the highest part of it was 20 feet above the sea. We had a glorious sleep for 12 hours, but through the night the northwest swell increased to a great height. The surrounding floes were hurled by the swell against our home, undermining

Under sail for Elephant Island. A painting by George Marston

it so that large pieces continuously broke off ... When we turned out we found that we had lost nearly half of our floeberg ... The swell had increased to a tremendous height and ... our temporary home was being swept away at an unpleasantly rapid rate. We saw that in a few hours our foothold would be cut from under us. We and the boats would be thrown into that seething mass of heaving floes ... The undermined banks broke away at such a rate that twice we had to draw the boats back into safety.'

Shackleton's account shows his concern for his men: 'The dawn of April 13 came clear and bright with occasional passing clouds. Most of the men were looking seriously worn and strained. Their lips were cracked and their eyes and eyelids showed red on their salt-encrusted faces. The beards of the younger men might have been those of patriarchs, for the frost and salt spray had made them white. I called the *Dudley Docker* alongside and found that the condition of the people there was no better than in the *James Caird*. Obviously we must make land quickly so I decided to run for Elephant Island ... We made our way through the lanes till

Elephant Island – mountains and glaciers

at noon we were suddenly spewed out of the pack into the open sea. Dark blue and sapphire green ran the seas. Our sails were soon up, and with a fair wind we moved over the waves like three Viking ships on the quest of a lost Atlantis. With the sheets well out and the sun shining bright above, we enjoyed for a few hours a sense of freedom and the magic of the sea.

'[Later:] I decided that it would be safer to heave to and wait for daylight ... I thought it possible that we might overrun our goal in the darkness. So we made a sea-anchor out of oars and hove to, the *Dudley Docker* in the lead, since she had the longest painter. The *James Caird* swung astern of the *Dudley Docker* and the *Stancomb Wills* again had the third place. Rest was not for us. During the greater part of the night the sprays broke over the boats and froze in masses of ice, which had to be broken away ... The temperature was below zero and the wind penetrated our clothes and chilled us unbearably. I doubted if all the men would survive that night.

'A magnificent sunrise heralded in what we hoped would be our last day in the boats ... We cast off our sea-anchor which had grown during the night to the thickness of telegraph poles and the ice had to be chipped clear ... In the full daylight Elephant Island showed cold and severe to the north-north-west ... on the bearing that Worsley had laid on ... All day, with a gentle breeze on our port bow we sailed and pulled through a clear sea ... About four o'clock a stiff breeze came up ahead and, blowing against the current, produced a choppy sea. During the next hour of hard pulling we made no progress at all.

'The *James Caird* now took the *Stancomb Wills* in tow, as we could carry more sail ... When darkness set in our goal was still some miles away. A heavy sea was running. It was a stern night. The men, except the watch, crouched and huddled in the bottom of the boat, getting what little warmth they could from the soaking sleeping bags and each other's bodies. Harder and harder blew the wind and fiercer and fiercer grew the sea. The boat plunged heavily through the squalls and came up to the wind.

'Towards midnight the wind shifted to the south-west, and this change enabled us to bear up closer to the island. A little later the *Dudley Docker* ran down to the *James Caird*, and Worsley shouted a suggestion that he should go ahead and search for a landing-place. His boat had the heels of the *James Caird* with the *Stancomb Wills* in tow. I told him he could try but he must not lose sight of the *James Caird*. Just as he left me a heavy snow-squall came down, and in the darkness the boats parted. I saw the *Dudley Docker* no more.'

Worsley explains the outcome: 'About midnight we lost sight of the *James Caird* ... but not long after saw the light of the *James Caird*'s compass-lamp, which Sir Ernest was flashing on their sail, as a guide to us ... By this time we had got into a bad tide-rip which, combined with the heavy, lumpy sea made it impossible to keep the *Dudley Docker* from swamping. As it was we shipped several bad seas over the stern as well as abeam and over the bows. [Earlier he explains]: Our freeboard was 1 ft 8 ins so our gunwale was only 20 inches above the sea in smooth weather.'

Two graphic descriptions emphasise the discomfort and hardship suffered during those six days of purgatory. The first is by Worsley: 'About two hours before dawn we were all shivering so badly that we huddled against each other for warmth, with the flimsy covering of the tent drawn up over us to keep off as much of the chill blast as we could. We lay on the stores at the bottom of the boat, bunched together in a chaotic mass, and if one unfortunate bedfellow on the outer edge moved a little, thus allowing the bitterly cold wind to get under the canvas, his immediate neighbours would wither him with the most scorching language I have ever heard. After a little time, however, I felt that I had had enough of the discomfort of it, so I crawled out and, standing in the stern of the boat, lit a cigarette and surveyed the scene. Shortly afterwards, Greenstreet followed me, and as we looked at the writhing tent and the extraordinary objects bumping about beneath it, we burst into yells of uncontrollable laughter.'

A. H. Macklin,[11] one of the ship's two doctors, who was sailing in the *Dudley Docker*, described the overcrowded conditions in the boats in telegraphese: 'Under way at last, large amount of bird life flew all around – annoyances of dropped excreta – whales blowing all round us – difficult rowing through the ice – thick and fouled the oars – rowing cold to fingers. *Dudley Docker* packed with food cases – stove – meat bag – sleeping bags under canvas in bow – paraffin – tent – clothing bags. Seats too low for rowing – sat on packing cases – not a satisfactory arrangement. Four oars and two spare ones – one mast and small lugsail. *Stancomb* and *Caird* also packed with provisions, tents etc. ... Skilful ice navigation by Sir E.'

Worsley again: 'The temperature was 20° below freezing

Landing on Elephant Island

... We were close to land as the morning approached but could see nothing of it through the snow and spindrift. At 3 a.m. Greenstreet relieved me at the tiller. I was so cramped from long hours, cold, and wet, in the constricted position one was forced to assume on top of the gear and stores, at the tiller, that the other men had to pull me amidships and straighten me out like a jack-knife ... By 8 a.m. ... I was able to keep her close in ... picking up lumps of fresh-water ice as we sailed through them. Our thirst was intense ... and we chewed fragments of ice with greedy relish.'

Shackleton in the *James Caird* takes up the story: 'At 9 a.m. at the north-west end of the island we saw a narrow beach at the end of the cliffs. Outside lay a fringe of rocks heavily beaten by the surf but with a narrow channel showing us a break in the foaming water. The *Stancomb Wills* was the lighter and handier boat and I called her alongside with the intention of taking her through the gap first and ascertaining the possibilities of a landing before the *James Caird* made the venture. I was just climbing into the *Stancomb Wills* when I saw the *Dudley Docker* coming up astern under sail. The sight took a great load off my mind.'

It was a very difficult landing, achieved in stages, but soon the three boats were ashore and safe. Shackleton then observes: 'When I landed the second time ... some of the men were reeling about the beach as if they had found an unlimited supply of alcoholic liquor on the desolate shore. They were laughing uproariously, picking up stones and letting handfuls of pebbles trickle through their fingers like misers gloating over hoarded gold.'

It was their first return to dry land since leaving South Georgia over sixteen months before. 'Soon half-a-dozen of us had the stores ashore. Our strength was nearly exhausted ... and we turned gratefully to enjoy the hot drink that the cook had prepared. Seal steak and blubber followed, for two seals had chosen to await our arrival ... There was no rest for the cook. The blubber stove flared and spluttered fiercely as he cooked, not one meal but many meals, which merged into a day-long bout of eating. We drank water and ate seal meat until every man had reached the limit of his capacity.'

It was 15 April 1916. Now they were castaways on an uninhabited island. No one knew where they were. The whale-hunters never called there. They had no radio.

The same day, Shackleton surveyed their beach and realised that spring tides and even a north-easterly gale would swamp their camp. A move was essential. Next morning he sent Wild, in the *Stancomb Wills*, to hunt for a more secure camp site along the north coast, and he returned with the

The three boats hauled up on the shore with a crowd round the *James Caird*

news that he had found a long sand spit 7 miles to the west, that would be suitable. A move was decided upon without delay, as Shackleton recounts: 'The morning of April 17 came fine and clear. By 11 a.m. we were away, with the *James Caird* leading ... Soon we were straining at the oars with the gale on our bows. Never had we found a more severe task.

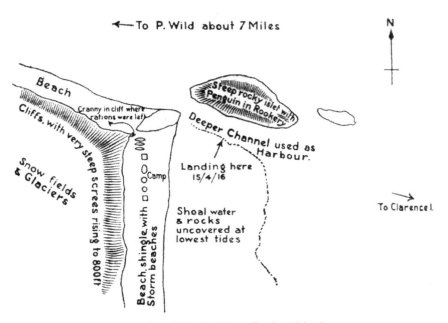

←—To P. Wild about 7 Miles

N

Beach

Cliffs, with very steep screes rising to 800ft

Cranny in cliff where rations were left

Snow fields & Glaciers

Steep rocky islet with Penguin in Rookery

Deeper Channel used as Harbour.

Landing here 15/4/16

Camp

Beach shingle, with Storm beaches

Shoal water & rocks uncovered at lowest tides

To Clarence I.

Point Valentine: the three boats' first landfall on Elephant Island

The wind shifted from the south to the south-west, and the shortage of oars became a serious matter.'

To launch the boats, they had had to use oars as rollers and had broken three: 'The *James Caird*, being the heaviest boat, had to keep a full complement of rowers, while the *Dudley Docker* and the *Stancomb Wills* went short and took turns using the odd oar. A big swell was thundering against the cliffs and at times we were almost driven onto the rocks by swirling green waters. We had to keep close inshore in order to avoid being embroiled in the raging sea, which was lashed snow-white and quickened by the furious swells into a living mass of sprays. After two hours of strenuous labour we were almost exhausted, but we were fortunate enough to find comparative shelter behind a point of rock ... The boats rose and fell in the big swell, but the sea was not breaking in our little haven, and we rested there while we ate our cold ration, but standing by to pole the boats off the cliff face.

'After half-an-hour's pause I gave the order to start again. The *Dudley Docker* was pulling with three oars, as the *Stancomb Wills* had the odd one, and she fell away to leeward in a particularly heavy squall ... All hands were wet to the skin again and many were feeling the cold severely. We forged on slowly and passed inside a great pillar of rock ... A line of reef stretched between the shore and the pillar ... but a break in the white surf revealed a gap in the reef and we laboured through, with the wind driving clouds of spray on our port beam. At last, about 5 p.m., the *James Caird* and the *Stancomb Wills* reached comparatively calm water and we saw Wild's beach just ahead of us.'

It had been a Herculean task, in lashing snowstorms and very heavy seas: 'During the first night the large eight-man tent blew to shreds in a violent gust of wind and they turned the *Dudley Docker* over, built a parapet round her with rocks and patched the holes with blankets. This was to serve as "home" for twenty-two men throughout the winter, which was already upon them.'

In retrospect, the events of the five months since the *Endurance* sank epitomise Shackleton's qualities of leadership. Here were 28 men who had lived in the open, entirely at the mercy of the elements: adrift for months on ice floes which were solid at first, but as the northward drift continued, began to break up and no longer offered a reliable platform for their camp and for their former activities. These floes then began to heave and rock about on the swell, and split up unexpectedly. As large floes drifted apart and then crashed together again their violence was tremendous. It was extremely unnerving and the uncertainties could have devastated morale. It was then that Shackleton came into his element. He seemed to thrive in these conditions, always devising competitions and entertainments, such as sing-songs and other diversions to keep everyone occupied. He never seemed at a loss and always had a plan to meet any eventuality. Apparently tireless and full of resource, he imbued his men with his display of self-confidence until they came to believe that he could overcome any crisis. Nevertheless, the supreme test was still to come.

5

PLANNING
THE RESCUE

Having organised the camp on Elephant Island as well as they could, the next problem was to effect a rescue. Worsley summed up the situation: 'Plainly the thing to do was to take a boat to the nearest inhabited point, risking the lives of a few for the preservation of the party. It was certain that a man of such heroic mind and self-sacrificing nature as Shackleton would undertake this most dangerous and difficult task himself. He was, in fact, by nature unable to do otherwise. Being a born leader, he had to lead in the position of most danger. I have seen him turn pale yet force himself into the post of greatest peril. That was his type of courage. He would do the job he was most afraid of.'

Worsley outlined their prospects of survival: 'The great unceasing westerly swell of the Southern Ocean rolls almost unchecked around this end of the world in the Roaring Forties and the Stormy Fifties. The highest, broadest and longest swells in the world, 400, 1,000 yards, a mile apart in fine weather, rising forty, fifty feet or more from crest to hollow, these blue water hills in a very heavy gale move 25 miles an hour and sometimes even fifty or more. Fast

Frank Worsley, the 'Skipper', a superb navigator

clippers, lofty ships and small craft are tossed on their foaming, snowy brows and stamped and battered by their ponderous feet, while the biggest liners are playthings for these real Leviathans of the Deep. Many a good ship has foundered with all hands; a tossing lifeboat or a grating alone remaining to mark their grave ... The westerly gales in the area that we proposed to cross are almost unceasing in the winter and cause strong east-running currents. That meant that we had practically no hope of reaching Cape Horn, very little of making the Falklands, but would have fair gales and favouring currents for South Georgia.'

Worsley had, in fact, worked out the courses and distances from the South Orkneys and from Elephant Island to these places even before *Endurance* was crushed and sunk, a remarkable example of prescience. The United States sailing instructions for Antarctica paint an even more alarming picture, warning mariners that: 'The winds are often of hurricane intensity with gust velocities sometimes attaining 150 to 200 miles per hour. Winds of such violence are not known elsewhere.' The risks inherent in sailing a small boat 800 miles to South Georgia in an Antarctic winter could not be overstated.

Shackleton, as usual in moments of decision, discussed the prospects with Worsley, his most trusted and experienced confidant, as the latter described later: 'The day dawned when Shackleton had to face the fact that he would not be able to feed his men through the winter. I remember that day. He asked me to walk with him to our usual lookout promontory, and there he confided to me his evergrowing anxiety.

'"Skipper" he said, "we shall have to make that boat journey, however risky it is. I am not going to let the men starve." Knowing what his presence meant to the others I hoped that he would remain in temporary but comparative safety on land and allow me to go in his stead. So I said, "would you let me take the boat?"

'"No," he replied, sharply, "that's my job."

'I told him that, after all, I had considerable experience in boating, surf-landings, and so on, and that in this respect I was really better equipped for the journey than he; but he stopped me by clapping me on the shoulder and saying, "Don't worry, Skipper, you'll be with me anyway." It was useless trying to persuade him to change his mind, for it was an integral part of his character to refrain from delegating responsibility ... Shackleton turned to me suddenly. "It's hateful having to tell the men that we've got to leave them," he said. "If things went wrong, it might be said that I had abandoned them."

'When Shackleton assembled the men they saw at once by his grave looks that he had made an important decision. Each man had noticed and been alarmed by the impending shortage of food ... Now he had come to the point when it was necessary to let them know everything. Gravely he explained the situation, and told them that he had determined to make a boat journey for help.

'"I'm afraid its a forlorn hope," he said, "and I don't ask anyone to come who has not thoroughly weighed the chances." The moment he ceased speaking every man volunteered.

'It was a dramatic scene and one that I am not likely to forget. On the island there was still safety for some weeks. The boat journey promised even worse hardships than those through which we had but recently passed. Yet so strong was the men's affection for Shackleton, so great was their loyalty to him, that they responded as though they had not undergone any of the experiences that so often destroy those sentiments.'

Shackleton chose the *James Caird* for the voyage as she was the largest and most seaworthy of the three boats. Originally she measured, internally, a mere 22 feet 6 inches

The Boss

long, 6 feet wide with a depth of 2 feet 4 inches. These dimensions had been increased when her sides were raised while on the ice, after *Endurance* sank, giving her a depth of 3 feet 7 inches. Despite these precautions, during the six-day voyage from the pack ice to Elephant Island the wind and waves were so violent that she constantly shipped seas over bows and stern, and the crew had to bail constantly. It was clear that something had to be done to improve the situation.

Shackleton writes: 'I walked through the blizzard with Worsley and Wild to examine the *James Caird*. The 20 foot boat had never looked big; she seemed to have shrunk in some mysterious way when I viewed her in the light of our new undertaking. She was an ordinary ship's whaler, fairly strong but showing signs of the strains she had endured since the crushing of the *Endurance*. Standing beside her, we glanced at the fringe of the storm-swept, tumultuous sea that formed our path. I called the carpenter and asked him if he could do anything to make the boat more seaworthy. He first enquired if he was to go with me, and seemed quite pleased when I said "yes" ... He had a good knowledge of sailing boats and was very quick. McCarthy [This is clearly a mistake for 'McNeish', the carpenter. McCarthy was an Able Seaman.] said that he could contrive some sort of covering for the *James Caird* if he might use the lids of the cases and the four sledge-runners that we had lashed inside the boat for use in the event of a landing on Graham Land at Wilhelmina Bay ... The carpenter proposed to complete the covering with some of our canvas, and he set about making his plans at once.

'Noon had passed and the gale was more severe than ever. We could not complete our preparations that day ... The gale was stronger than ever next morning (Apr. 20). No work could be done. Blizzard and snow, snow and blizzard, sudden lulls and fierce returns. There was a lull in the bad weather on April 21st, and he started to collect material for the decking of the *James Caird*. He fitted the mast from the *Stancomb Wills* fore and aft, inside the *James Caird* along the keel to strengthen it and prevent it from buckling in heavy seas. By using sledge-runners and box-lids he made a framework extending aft from the forecastle to the well. We

Frank Wild

had a bolt of canvas frozen stiff, to be sewn into the form of a cover. We certainly could not have lived through the voyage without it.'

Greenstreet

Bakewell

Worsley's account is more colourful: 'Frozen like a board and caked with ice, the canvas was sewn in painful circumstances, by two cheery optimists, Greenstreet, Chief Officer of the *Endurance* and Bakewell, a Canadian AB.[12] The only way they could do it was by holding the frozen canvas in the blubber fire till it thawed, often burning their fingers, while the oily smoke got in their eyes and noses, half-blinding and choking them. Then they sewed, often getting frost-bitten and having to use great care that the difficult sewing with cold, brittle sail needles did not break all our scanty supply. All the time, while repeating the unpleasant task of thawing out a length, "Horace" was irrepressibly cracking his sailor jokes and Bakewell replying.'

In addition to the sledge-runners, Worsley states that McNeish took timbers from the *Dudley Docker* for the decking and that a mast and sail from the *Stancomb Wills* were cut down to make a mizzen mast and sail for the *James Caird*, but, according to his diary entry for 25 November 1915, this was done while the expedition was in Ocean Camp, several months before. The illustration 'Under sail for Elephant Island' in Shackleton's book *South*, showing her with a mizzen mast before they reached Elephant Island, tends to confirm this. She was thus rigged as a ketch, with a jib, a standing lugsail with a loose foot (no boom) on the mainmast and a standing lugsail, but with a boom, on the mizzen mast.

Preparing the *James Caird*

McNeish pressed on with decking and rigging the *James Caird* whenever the gales and snowstorms permitted. Without any protection of any kind, this was a remarkable labour. By the time he had finished, all her dimensions had been increased, so that she measured 23 feet 6 inches long, 7 feet 3 inches in the beam and 4 feet 7 inches deep. She had a cockpit or well, measuring 5 feet by 2 feet 6 inches, forward of the mizzen mast. Having no ballast keel, she was ballasted, according to Worsley, with 'about fifteen hundredweight of shingle ballast ... in canvas bags, with another five hundredweight of large stones.' He puts her freeboard, height above the waterline, as 2 feet 2 inches.

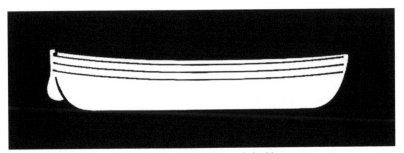

The hull of the *James Caird* with extra strakes and decking

The sail plan, with the mizzen on the left

This does not agree with Shackleton's account in *South*: 'The ballast consisted of bags made from blankets and filled with sand, a total weight of about 1,000 lbs. In addition we had gathered a supply of round boulders and about 250 lbs of ice.' 'He and I [wrote Worsley in his book *Endurance*], were not in agreement about the amount of ballast. I wanted him to use only little more than half of the amount upon which he had decided, ... but, filled with the dread of being under-ballasted, he insisted on having more than a ton. The result of this was that we were lower in the water than I liked to be. Later on, Shackleton said to me: "Skipper, you were right. I made a mistake about the ballast. Had I listened to you, I think the journey would have been shorter, the boat wouldn't have been so stiff or so jumpy in her movements, and we would have shipped very few heavy seas. I'm sorry." Not every leader, after he had brought his men safely through, would have conceded that he had made even a small mistake.'

Worsley was also unhappy with the rig: 'I would have preferred the jib and lug only, the latter with a long foot. Ship's boats grip [gripe?] to windward and the mizen, when set, kept her so much in the wind that the rudder was always dragged across to keep her off; it was in the way, forced us to use a yoke [with two ropes] instead of a tiller [that is, with a bar] and, being a third sail, was a source of misery, especially when it and its gear got iced up. The shrouds of the mainmast were secured with four brass screws, two inches long. The boat's gear consisted of four oars, six crutches, a long rope for a painter and dragging the sea anchor, a Navy boat's compass, an oil bag, red lights, flaming matches, two water breakers [kegs], a baler, two axes, a marlin-spike, and a repair bag.'

In addition to these, the meticulous Shackleton listed the instruments, stores, and food rations carried, to last six men for one month (see box on next page).

Shackleton then had to make another vital decision: whom to take with him and whom to leave in charge on Elephant Island. To command the main party he chose Frank Wild, the wiry, tough companion of his attempt on the South Pole, eight years before. He could rely on his experience, initiative, unbounded energy and will to survive, to see them through. To go with him, his first choice was Frank Worsley, Master of *Endurance*, exceptionally tough and a first-rate navigator on whose unswerving loyalty he could rely. Next

SHACKLETON'S LIST OF BOAT STORES

30 boxes of matches
6½ gallons paraffin
1 tin methylated spirit
10 boxes of flamers (burners)
1 box of blue lights
2 Primus stoves with spare parts and prickers
1 Nansen aluminium cooker
6 sleeping bags
A few spare socks
A few candles and some blubber-oil in an oil-bag

Food

3 cases sledging rations = 300 rations
2 cases nut food = 200 rations
2 cases biscuits = 600 biscuits
1 case lump sugar
30 packets of Trumilk
1 tin of Bovril cubes
1 tin of Cerebos salt
36 gallons of water
112 lb ice

Instruments

Sextant
Binoculars
Prismatic compass
Sea anchor
Charts
Aneroid

Tom Crean

he picked Tom Crean, his Second Officer, Irish to the core
and as strong as an ox. He took three more: Tim McCarthy,
another Irishman and an irrepressible optimist; the Scots
carpenter, Harry McNeish, whose skills would be of more
use in the boat than on Elephant Island; and finally, 'Bosun'
Vincent, a former trawler hand. He had a second reason for
choosing the last two. He regarded both as trouble-makers,

Preparing to launch the *James Caird*

Launching the *James Caird*

The *James Caird* awaits loading

The *James Caird* leaves Elephant Island for South Georgia

who would be better with him than with Wild. Later, neither was recommended for a Polar Medal.

They all knew, as Shackleton wrote later, that: 'the perils of the proposed journey were extreme. The ocean south of Cape Horn in the middle of May is known to be the most tempestuous, storm-swept area of water in the world, The tale of the next 17 days is one of supreme strife and heaving waters. The sub-Antarctic Ocean lived up to its evil reputation.'

After a week on Elephant Island, work on the *James Caird* was completed and Shackleton was anxious to get away before the worst of the winter set in. They planned to leave on 24 April and by good fortune it dawned sunny, calm and almost perfect for the start. A clear prospect of the horizon enabled Worsley to rate his chronometer and obtain a good view of a gap in the ring of loose ice, which almost circled the island. The *James Caird* was hauled down to the sea and launched but was at once hit by a roller and nearly capsized, throwing McNeish and Vincent into the sea. They were pulled out quickly, and the two men given a change of clothing. The boat was anchored, but then Worsley found that she was half-full of water, as the plug had been knocked out of her bottom. Putting in a temporary stopper, he and McCarthy baled her dry, found the missing plug and replaced it. The ballast was then ferried out and stowed, followed by the stores, gear, sleeping bags, and food supplies. One of the water kegs was damaged on a rock and, unfortunately, no one realised that sea water had leaked in.

6

SHACKLETON'S BOAT JOURNEY

At midday on 24 April 1916 Shackleton set a course through the Drake Passage, a name to bring dread even to seasoned mariners. South Georgia was a distant speck beyond the Scotia Sea. They might sail right past it if their navigation was slightly out. Only rarely did the sun appear to enable them to fix their position, an extremely difficult task from the deck of a small boat that heaved constantly. In the event, Worsley's accuracy was quite remarkable.

In retrospect, Worsley grew quite lyrical at leaving the land: 'Elephant Island was opening up astern in majesty of snow peaks and uplands, fronted by glacier walls and towering cliffs. To the east, Cornwallis and Clarence Islands were revealed – two beautiful, serene, and stately virgins – with soft, mauve wreaths and veils of misty clouds around their brows and shoulders. Around us droves of gentoo penguins, with a few seals ... Great fragments and hummocks of very old floes ... rose and fell on the heaving sea, drawing deceptively apart, then closing with a thud that would have smashed our boat like a gas mantle between thumb and finger. Castles, towers and churches swayed

Floating bergs almost surrounded Elephant Island

unsteadily around us. Small pieces gathered and rattled against the boat.'

Once more the Boss's luck held. 'How opportunely Shackleton's departure was timed,' wrote Hurley in his journal (he was one of those who remained on Elephant Island), 'may be gathered from the fact that the next morning a shift of wind filled the bay with pack ice, blocking all access to the sea for many weeks.'

On the first night they steered by the Southern Cross, which was visible through broken cloud. At dawn an albatross appeared from nowhere. For two days they sailed north to clear the ice floes, but on the third, they changed course to the north-east and made 83 miles. Worsley managed to get an observation of the sun but it took four men to achieve it. As he knelt on the after-thwart with his sextant, two men held on to him, one on either side, while Shackleton crouched under cover with the chronometer, pencil and paper, as the boat pitched, rolled and jerked heavily. Worsley describes it: 'As the boat leapt frantically upward on the crest of a wave, I snapped a good guess at the altitude and shouted "Stop". The Boss took the time and I worked out the result. Then the fun started. Our fingers were so cold that he had to interpret his wobbly figures – my own so illegible that I had to recognise them by feats of memory.'

He explains that his navigating books had become soaked and sodden, with the pages stuck together, the figures nearly illegible and everything almost reduced to pulp.

They worked four-hour watches, three men to each, in conditions described by Shackleton: 'The discomfort of life in the *James Caird* was extreme. There was little room to move. Cramped in our narrow quarters and continually wet by spray, we suffered severely throughout the journey. Icy trickles and driving spray poured fore and aft into the boat and we bailed non-stop. Of real rest we had none. The perpetual motion of the boat made repose impossible; we were cold, sore and anxious. We moved on hands and knees in the semi-darkness of the day, under the decking.'

A biographer[13] who interviewed some of the survivors, elaborates: 'They were already exhausted with the dreadful year of winter. Their clothes were worn and tattered, their skin flayed at every joint with the horrible sea-blisters which salt water, cold and the friction of rough clothes produce. They could not stand up except for a moment or so; they could not lie down except on the rough angles of the ballast and the cases under the dripping canvas deck; they could not even sit, except in the open well, at the stern, where the steersman was often so cramped that he could not unbend his knees or lift his hands, when relieved.'

Shackleton continues: 'A severe south-westerly gale forced us to heave to on the fourth day. The sea was very high and the *James Caird* was in danger of broaching to [turning sideways to the seas] and swamping. We hove to under

Streaming the sea anchor

double-reefed mainsail and our little jigger and waited for the gale to blow itself out. On the fifth day the gale was so fierce that we were compelled to take in the mainsail and hoist our small jib instead. We put out a sea-anchor to keep the *James Caird*'s head up to the sea. This anchor consists of a conical canvas bag, wider at one end than the other [a 'venturi' effect], fastened to the end of a painter [a rope] and allowed to stream out from the bows, to act as a kind of brake. The boat was high enough to catch the wind and, as she drifted to leeward, the drag of the anchor kept her head to windward. Thus our boat took the seas more or less, end on. Even then the crests of the waves would often curl right over us and we shipped a great deal of water which necessitated unceasing bailing and pumping. That day, we made a mere 18 miles of drift.'

On the sixth day it blew a west-south-west gale and they made a fine run of 92 miles. That made 238 miles covered since leaving Elephant Island. Worsley managed to get another position by the sun, and takes up the story: 'It blew a heavy southwest by west gale on the last day of April. A heavy sea was making up, before which the boat ran badly, steering wildly and shipping heavy seas until noon,

Shooting the sun

Working out the result

when we had to heave to and pay out the sea anchor. After this she took very little water. The run was 78 miles by dead reckoning.'

When May Day dawned on the eighth day out, they found themselves in a perilous situation. According to Worsley: 'We found the boat riding deep in the water, and liable to capsize, the ice on her being so thick and heavy. Something had to be done and quickly. We took it in turns to creep out with an axe and chop the ice off. What a job! The boat leapt and

Chopping off the ice

kicked like a mule. She was covered 15 inches deep in a casing of ice with slush all over where the last sea was freezing. First you chopped a hand-hold, then a knee-hold and then chopped off ice hastily while a sea washed over you. After five minutes, you slid back into shelter and the next man took over. If a man had gone overboard it would have been goodbye. Twice more that day, we had to do it all over again.

'Once, as the boat gave a tremendous lurch, I saw Vincent slide right across the icy sheathing of the canvas, and, horror-stricken, I threw myself instinctively to help him, only to find that he was beyond my reach. Fortunately he was able to grasp the mast just as he was going overboard.'

Throughout the voyage Shackleton kept an eagle eye on the morale and well-being of his crew, while they were very conscious of his concern for them. He well knew that regular meals of hot food were vital for their survival. Their food preparation must have been a strange sight, for two men had

Cooking the 'hoosh'

A Primus stove with Nansen attachment

to brace their backs against the sides of the boat, with the Primus jammed between their feet to keep it upright, one balancing the cooking pot as the boat leapt about and sometimes stood on end. Worsley describes how matters were organised: 'At this time we were living on rations devised by Shackleton in conjunction with Sir William Beveridge, the Army food expert. The principal article of our diet was a mixture that looked like a dark brown brick, which consisted of beef protein, lard, oatmeal, sugar and salt. This was cooked over the Primus to a thick mixture resembling pea-soup. Every four hours in the daytime we had a meal of this, which we took scalding hot. Sometimes after this "hoosh", as Shackleton called it, we would have a half-pound block of Streimer's Nut Food, a food of the nougat type, extremely sweet, which, however, never cloyed our appetites down there ... In between meals, if Shackleton thought we needed a morale booster, of some kind, he would suddenly issue a block of this, or half-a-dozen lumps of sugar and a biscuit of a specially nourishing kind that he had prepared for his sledging trips. It was a matter of principle with him to feed everybody to the greatest possible extent, so as to give them reserves with which to overcome the cold and wet.'

One of Shackleton's main concerns throughout the expedition had been to avoid scurvy, that 'killer', dreaded by sailing ships' crews and explorers. He never forgot his experience in 1902 during their southern journey when he, Scott and Wilson all suffered from it. On this occasion his precautions proved completely successful.

It is almost inconceivable that they could have survived without that remarkable Swedish invention, the Primus stove, which they used for cooking and, on occasion, for heating. The Norwegian explorer Nansen designed a hollow cylindrical drum, or water-jacket, which fitted over it, providing a container for melting snow. Worsley explains: 'The few miserable rays of light that penetrated the gloom, served only to accentuate the wretchedness of our condition. Shackleton, seeing that we all needed gingering up, told Crean to light the little Primus cooker, so that we could sit round it and talk and smoke for a bit. If you light a Primus stove in an ordinarily heated room, you will notice very little difference in the temperature; but even the small amount that it threw out and the slight diminution of bitter cold that resulted, was of psychological value to us, for it gave us the impression that we were warm, consequently comfortable, and to go a little further, comparatively happy. For two hours we smoked, yarned and coughed in the acrid fumes of the Primus, until the three men who had got into their sleeping bags had dozed off. Then the stern necessity of conserving

Cramped in the cockpit

fuel being ever present, the Primus was put out.'

Worsley described the problems of 'watch below' under the decking: 'Our sleeping bags were laid in the bows on top of food boxes, whose sharp corners stuck into our bodies in inconvenient and painful fashion. It was a strange cabin, seven feet long, five feet wide at one end, tapering to a point at the other. Barely room to sit up, after crawling in through the narrow space between the ballast and the thwart above. What a crawl! It became a nightmare. The first part on hands and knees over sharp stones ... which you slipped off and on ... You braced yourself up – or rather down – crawling and wriggling on chest and stomach ... Halfway through you paused for breath ... but then came a gentle nudge from the next man's head or shoulder against your after-end, and you again moved reluctantly forward ... Here we were lifted up and hurled down. With her bows and our bodies we whipped, swept, flailed and stamped on the seas ... We leaped on the swells, danced on them, flew over them, and dived into them. We wagged like a dog's tail, shook like a

The *James Caird* in a gale – a painting by Norman Wilkinson owned by Dulwich College

flag in a gale, and switchbacked over hills and dales. We were sore all over.'

They had other problems: 'We all steered, reefed, furled or set sail, and pumped in turns. One man had to hold down the pump's brass tube in ice-cold water at the bottom of the boat, while the other man worked the plunger up and down. The man holding the tube down had to use force to prevent the other man pulling it out of his hands. Our hands were unable, even slightly, to warm the tube, as there was a constant stream of cold water up inside. The seas that swept over us had to be pumped out every four hours – often every two – and between whiles we heard the water running about under the ballast in an alarming manner ... and at all hours the iron rod of the pump was working up and down within a few inches of the compass. However, with this style of navigation I got some surprisingly accurate results.'

Worsley hints at the variety of events that helped to keep them going: 'We saw a few penguins in the afternoon, 300

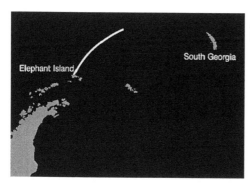

Almost halfway to South Georgia

miles from any land. They were quite indifferent to the gale or the cold; we felt envious of them ... We drank seal oil, black and odiferous ... its calories were so valuable ... Sir Ernest had the Primus going day and night as long as we could stand the fumes, then it would be put out for an hour ... All gear was wet through and the sleeping bags had a nasty, sour-bread kind of smell and were on the point of fermenting. I believe, in fact, that some fermenting had started, and so prevented us feeling the cold so much in our sleep, as we called it. We all smelt as well, or rather as ill, as our bags. We used to long for a hot bath or clean, dry clothes.'

On the ninth day, 2 May, they lost their sea anchor, as Worsley recounts: 'In the forenoon a heavy sea struck the *Caird*. Almost immediately her bows fell off till the sea was abeam. The great cake of ice that had formed on the painter at the bows, which we could not smash off, had sawed and chafed through it. So we lost both rope and sea-anchor, a double disaster for us. We beat the ice off the jib, reefed and set it on the mainmast. By then the gale had eased enough for us to set the reefed lug and jib and run drunkenly before the wind and sea. While hove to I reckoned we had drifted 66 miles ... After my "trick" at the helm in the middle watch, when extra cold and wet, I got stiffened in the crouching position I had assumed to dodge the seas, and had to be hauled inside, massaged, and opened out like a jack-knife, before I could get into my sleeping bag.'

On the tenth day the south-west gale moderated, the sun came out and Worsley obtained another fix for position. The day's run was 62 miles, putting them 444 miles from Elephant Island. The *Caird* was over halfway to South Georgia. Worsley describes the day: 'The weather became bright and clear with splendid warming spells of sunshine that we revelled in. It was the first good day of the passage. The few seas shipped we managed to dodge. We slung the sleeping bags and our clothing on the masts, halliards and rigging, which altered their condition from wet to damp. We were a ragged, tough-looking crew of cut-throat appearance. We didn't care, we were happy.'

The eleventh day brought a modest south-west breeze and a moderate sea. Worsley managed to get another shot of the sun as the boat leaped high on a crest. That day they ran 52 miles, making a total of 496 miles, and they were able to hang their bedding out again. Day 12 was clear but overcast, the wind was squally with a lumpy sea but a good south-west breeze gave them a run of 96 miles, their best to date.

But, all at once, the *James Caird* was nearly overwhelmed, as Shackleton describes: 'At midnight on the fifth of May, I was at the tiller and suddenly noticed a line of clear sky between south and south-west. A moment later I realised that it was the white crest of an enormous wave. During twenty-six years' experience, I had not encountered a wave so gigantic. It was a mighty upheaval of the ocean, quite apart from the big white-capped seas that had been our tireless enemies for days. I shouted "for God's sake hold on". We felt our boat lifted and flung forward like a cork in a breaking surf. Somehow it lived through it, half full of water, sagging to the dead weight and shuddering under the blow. We baled with the energy of men fighting for life.'

Worsley, as usual, is more graphic in his descriptions: 'The

The enormous wave

The *James Caird* engulfed in the wave

boat seemed full of water. We other five men seized any receptacle we could find and pushed, scooped, and baled the water out for dear life. While Shackleton held her up to the wind, we worked like madmen. With the aid of the little home-made pump and two dippers it took us nearly an hour to get rid of the water. The wave that had struck us was so sudden and enormous ... that it may have been caused by the capsizing of some great iceberg.'

Later that day a north-by-west gale forced them to heave to with reefed jib on the mainmast. A short glimpse of the sun enabled Worsley to fix their position at 100 miles from South Georgia.

Meanwhile, life in the *James Caird* was not all misery, as Worsley suggests: 'In some of the few fine watches that we had, Crean made noises at the helm, that, we surmised, represented "The Wearin' o' the Green". Another series of sounds completely baffled us. I sang:

> She licked him, she kicked him,
> She wouldn't let him be;
> She welted him, she belted him,
> Until he couldn't see.
> But Macarty wasn't hearty;
> Now she's got a different party.
> She might have licked Macarty,
> But she can't *lick me*.

'The last part to Macarty.[14] [*sic*] Then I sang: "We're bound for the Rio Grande!" No one complained.'

Learning from experience, Worsley developed more sophisticated ways of taking a sun sight: 'The day before, I had taken observations of the sun, cuddling the mast with one arm and swinging fore and aft round the mast, sextant and all. This day I found the best way was to sit on the deck, to jam one foot between the mast and halyards, the other against the shroud, and catch the sun when the boat leaped her highest on the crest of a sea, allowing the "height of eye" accordingly ... Since leaving Elephant Island I had only been able to get the sun four times, two of these being mere snaps or guesses through slight rifts in the clouds. Making the land

... the conditions for observing the sun were most unfavourable. It was misty, the boat was jumping like a flea, shipping seas fore and aft, and there was no "limb" to the sun, so I had to observe the centre by guesswork.'

Now that the *James Caird* was closing on South Georgia, Shackleton decided to set course for the south side of the island. Although the whaling stations of Grytviken and Stromness were on the north-east coast, he was afraid of missing the land in bad visibility. Then another problem faced him. Sea water had leaked into their last keg of drinking water; it seems that it had been damaged when the boat was loaded. Although they strained it through a piece of medicated gauze to get rid of sediment and reindeer hair – from the sleeping bags – it was still brackish. They were now rationed to one gill (quarter of a pint) per day and their hot milk at night had to be stopped. They had not seen any ice floating on the sea for days. Shackleton explained what that meant to them: 'Thirst took possession of us but I dared not increase the allowance of water. Lack of water is the most severe privation that men can be condemned to endure. Salt water in our clothing and the salt water that lashed our faces made our thirst grow quickly to a burning pain. Our mouths were dry and our tongues swollen. We did our work dully and hoped for land.

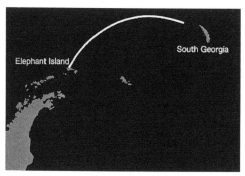

Almost there

Landfall on Cape Demidov. A painting by George Marston

'The morning of May 8th broke thick and stormy, with squalls from the north-west. About eleven o'clock we saw two shags sitting on a big mass of kelp, and knew we must be within ten or fifteen miles of the shore, for these birds never venture far to sea. At 12.30, through a rift in the clouds, McCarthy caught a glimpse of the black cliffs of South Georgia with a shout of "land-ho"! It was Cape Demidov. It was superb navigation'

They all thought their voyage was nearly over, but the elements had by no means finished with them. They had many glimpses of the rocky coast but it was too rough to approach. As night came, they hove the *James Caird* to, some 18 miles off shore, as it was blowing a hard gale with rain, snow, sleet and hail. They waited for morning and Worsley takes up the story: 'At daybreak on the 9th of May, we were wallowing in a terribly heavy cross-sea, with a mountainous westerly swell setting us onto the coast, before the furious,

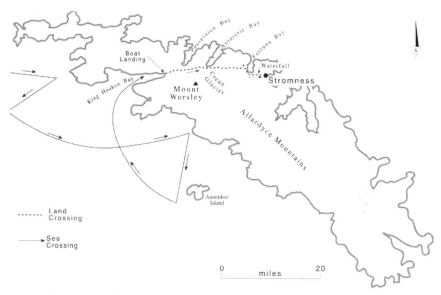

Approach to South Georgia

westerly gale then raging. Half the time our view was obscured by thick, driving misty squalls. By noon the gale had risen to hurricane force and was driving us harder than ever, straight for that iron-bound coast. We remained hove to until two o'clock when, through a sudden rift in the storm-driven clouds, we saw two high, jagged crags and a line of precipitous cliffs on our lee quarter. We were being blown on shore onto the stretch between King Haakon Sound and Annenkov Island. On each sea the boat swept upward till she heeled before the droning fury of the hurricane, then fell staggering into the hollow, almost becalmed. It was a most awe-inspiring and dangerous position ... While one steered three worked the pump, one baled with the two-gallon hoosh pot and the sixth stood by to relieve one of the others.

'An eight-mile-long reef was marked between Annenkov and South Georgia. We caught glimpses of it and others not charted and held on to wind'ard. Our chart, imperfect at best, was almost illegible from sea stains ... the island came so close we had to crane our necks to look up at the peak ... I believe some eddy of the tide or current drove us clear. Foot by foot we staggered and lurched drunkenly past the ravening black fangs of the rocky point. With infinite difficulty and danger of being washed overboard we got the reefed jib off the main, set it for'ard, set reefed lug and mizzen, and with these large handkerchiefs, endeavoured to claw off shore, hoping to heaven that the mast would stand it. The strains, shocks and blows were tremendous as she struck an on-rushing sea, that swept her fore and aft even to the mastheads. Good boat! But how she stood it was a miracle.'

They heard later that a 500-ton steamer from Buenos Aires to South Georgia had foundered with all hands in that nine-hour-long hurricane: 'In striving to claw off the shore the boat struck the seas with a series of shocks as though she was beating herself against stone walls. ... The bow-planks on each side opened and closed, so that long lines of water squirted into her. She was soon leaking all over from the tremendous strain, and this, added to the seas which swept continuously over us, filled the boat to such an extent that three men working the pump were not enough. Two men had to bale at the same time as the others were pumping. Only by strenuous efforts did we prevent the boat from foundering beneath us.'

Shackleton takes up the final sequence of events: 'We could gauge our approach to the unseen cliffs by the roar of the breakers against the sheer walls of rock ... The afternoon wore away as we edged along the coast, with the thunder of the breakers in our ears. The chance of survival that night with the driving gale and the implacable sea forcing us onto the lee shore seemed small, I think most of us had the feeling that the end was near. Then, just when things looked their worst, they changed for the best ... The wind suddenly shifted and we were free once more to make an offing. Almost as soon as the gale eased, the pin that locked the mast

The cliffs of South Georgia

Annenkov Island

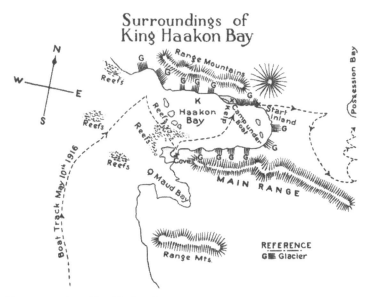

The approach to King Haakon Bay

to the thwart fell out. It must have been on the point of doing this throughout the hurricane.'

Worsley is more specific on this incident: 'Crean, crawling from his sleeping bag under the thwart, struck it with his shoulder. The pin that held the mast clamp in place must have worked upwards during the hurricane, till the point alone held. The slight shock from Crean's shoulder knocked it out. The clamp swung open, and the mast started to fall aft, but Macarty caught it and clamped and secured it with the pin. Happening then it was a trifling incident, but the pin had probably held in that precarious position all night. Had it fallen out in the hurricane, the mast would have snapped like a carrot, and no power on earth could have saved us.'

'When dawn came on May 10th,' Shackleton continues, 'there was a high cross-sea running. The wind backed to the north-west and we sighted what I thought was King Haakon Bay. We set the bows towards it and ran before the freshening gale. About noon we sighted a line of jagged reef, like

The 'jagged reef like blackened teeth' on left, seen from above King Haakon Bay, c. 1960s

blackened teeth, that seemed to be the entrance to the bay. A gap in the reef appeared and we made for it. But the wind shifted and blew us right out again. That afternoon we tacked for four hours into the strong wind. After five tacks the last one took us through ... I stood in the bows directing the steering. The entrance was so narrow, we had to take in the oars. In a minute or two we were inside and the *James Caird* ran into a cove on a swell and touched the beach. I sprang ashore with a short painter and in a few minutes we were all safe on the beach. We heard a jingly sound and found a stream of fresh water at our feet. In a moment we were down on our knees drinking the ice-cold water in long draughts that put new life into us.'

Clambering up a low cliff with the rope, Shackleton's legs were so weak from lack of exercise in the *Caird* that he fell and hurt himself, luckily not badly. The others were in a

Cape Rosa where the *James Caird* landed is revisited

similar state. Meanwhile they were unable to prevent the boat from bumping on the boulders in the swell but fortunately the planking withstood the battering. Their rudder became unshipped and floated away in the darkness, but three days later it floated back. Crean found a shallow cave, some 8 feet deep and 12 feet wide, hollowed out of the cliff face, which provided shelter from the elements. The entrance was draped with huge icicles, some 15 feet long. They even lit a fire inside it. That night they slept on solid ground at last.

Worsley describes the difficulties then faced by this group of exhausted and weakened men: '... it was imperative to haul the boat up out of the sea to prevent her from getting smashed. To do this we were obliged to throw out of her

A fanciful idea of how the *Caird* was hauled ashore. A painting by George Marston

every atom of gear and stores as quickly as possible. We formed a chain and handed the stuff ashore ... we had almost lost the use of our limbs through the continuous wetting and lack of normal movement due to the confined space on the boat ... we had not been able to sit upright for a meal, so that every muscle was cramped and we were in the condition that one might expect to find in sick or bedridden men.

'... Taking it in turn to watch the boat we snatched such sleep as we could until two o'clock in the morning. Then Crean, who was hanging on to the painter, gave a shout. We all rushed out, and, stumbling in the darkness to his help, found that a big sea had torn from the ground the boulder to which the painter was secured, and that Crean, hanging onto it, had been dragged into the water which threatened to submerge him. There was no more sleep. All hands had to hold onto the boat for the rest of the night.'

The next morning they set about securing the *James Caird* above tidemark; exhausting work according to Worsley: 'Then we set seriously to work to get the boat up the beach. The tide here rises only three feet, but at high water we hauled her as far as we could. We had not rope enough to rig a purchase, so we placed the two masts and a spare mast under her keel and worked her uphill. Boulders sticking up in our course hindered ... Then we got her onto a patch of shingle, where, using the masts as rollers, we hauled her diagonally and zig-zag up the incline, until we got her in safety on the tussocks. Had we been fit and strong, we could have got the boat up with an hour's hard work. As it was it took us from daylight to dark and it exhausted us.'

Worsley's rough log then reads: 'Thursday 11th May 1916. Camped in a small cave; dried some clothes and began to cut *Caird* down, she being so heavy we could not handle her or haul her clear of the surf. Noon: hauled boat clear of surf. Friday 12th: cutting down *Caird*. Saturday 13th: preparing *Caird* for pulling up to head of bay. There was ice in the cove for three days, so that we were detained in the cave for six days in all. Then some change in conditions swept the ice out of the cove. To see it leaving was an impressive and curious sight; it was like watching an army in full retreat.'

With the thought of the twenty-two men marooned on Elephant Island, dependent on him for their rescue, Shackleton was determined to press on. Worsley, Crean and

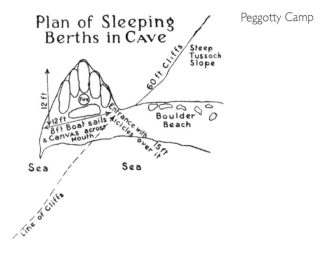

King Haakon Bay looking west

Peggotty Bluff

he wanted to find out what lay ahead of them, but were still too weak to investigate very far. They built up their strength feasting on succulent albatross chicks, which were nesting nearby. One chick could weigh up to 14 lb and these they mixed in their hoosh to help them face up to the ordeal that lay ahead. 'We did not enjoy attacking these birds but our hunger knew no law,' wrote Shackleton. 'They tasted so very good and assisted our recuperation.'

They also found a supply of timber washed up from wrecked ships to supplement their meagre fuel supply – mainly the topsides of the *Caird*. Worsley fixed their latitude at 54° 12' South – which did not tally with their German chart. In *South*, Shackleton describes King Haakon Bay as: '... a magnificent sight ... [but] its green waters were being beaten to fury by the north westerly gale. The mountains ... peered through the mists and between them huge glaciers poured down from the great ice-slopes and fields that lay behind. We counted twelve glaciers and heard every few minutes the reverberating roar caused by masses of ice calving from the parent streams ... May 15th was a great day. We made our hoosh at 7.30 a.m., then we loaded up the boat and gave her a flying launch down the steep beach into the surf. Heavy rain had fallen during the night and a gusty north-westerly wind was now blowing, with misty showers. The *James Caird* headed to the sea as if anxious to face the battle of the waves once more. We passed through the narrow mouth of the cove with the ugly rocks and waving kelp close on either side, turned to the east and sailed merrily up the bay as the sun broke through the mists and made the tossing waters sparkle around us ... The surf was sufficient to have endangered the boat if we had attempted to land ... We rounded a high, glacier-worn bluff on the north side, and at 12.30 p.m., we ran the boat ashore on a low beach of sand and pebbles, with tussock growing well above sea level ... We hauled the *James Caird* up above high water mark and turned her over just to the lee or east side of the bluff ... Soon we had converted the boat into a very comfortable cabin *à la* Peggotty, turfing it round with tussocks, which we dug up with knives. One side of the *James Caird* rested on stones so as to afford a low entrance, and when we had finished she looked as if she had grown there.'

7

THE CLIMB ACROSS
SOUTH GEORGIA

They were now camped near the head of King Haakon Bay, on the opposite side of South Georgia to the whaling stations at Leith, Husvik and Stromness. Shackleton had already abandoned any idea of trying to sail the *James Caird* round the east end of the island, a distance of 150 miles or so. By then the boat had been stripped down and was no longer fit for such a voyage. The alternative was to climb over the mountainous interior, a feat that had never even been attempted before. It was a wilderness of ice-bound peaks, the highest being Mount Paget at 9,000 feet, glaciers and snowfields, all unmapped and averaging 3,000 feet in height.

Such a climb would have been a daunting prospect even for experienced and well-equipped mountaineers. Shackleton and his companions were neither. In threadbare clothes, lacking proper climbing boots and in poor physical condition it would have been a foolhardy enterprise in any other circumstances. For them there was no choice if they were to survive and save the men on Elephant Island. Everything would depend on the weather. From their chart, Worsley reckoned that the direct route to Husvik was 17 miles, but they could not expect to follow a direct line.

To go with him Shackleton chose Worsley and Crean. To help give them a grip on the ice, McNeish put brass screws, taken out of the *James Caird*, in the soles of their finneskoe – their Lapp reindeer boots. Shackleton outlined their equipment for the journey: 'We would take three days' provisions for each man in the form of sledging ration and biscuit. The food was to be packed in three socks, so that each member of the party carried his own. Then we were to take the Primus lamp filled with oil, the small cooker, the carpenter's adze (for use as an ice-axe), the alpine rope, which made a total length of fifty feet when knotted.' They also took the log of the *Endurance*.

Worsley gives his own list of the equipment that he carried. It suggests that he saw himself as the expedition beast of burden, and raises the question – what did the other two carry apart from their socks of food? Worsley wrote: 'I carried two compasses, binoculars, the Alpine rope, and the chronometer with which I had navigated the boat. The last was slung round my neck inside my sweater to keep it warm. I remember my load very well, because I felt half-strangled with the four cords and straps round my throat, even before the addition of the coils of the ninety-foot Alpine rope.'

In Worsley's memory the rope has apparently grown by 40 feet and probably felt like 90 feet when it was round his shoulders.

In the event, Shackleton's proverbial luck held. No one deserved it more than he. The weather was fine and clear, with a full moon at night. They learned later that they had the advantage of the only fine period in a severe winter. They had to find their way round steep precipices, frequently back-tracking as they hunted for a safe route around obstacles. Once they were completely stuck and Shackleton

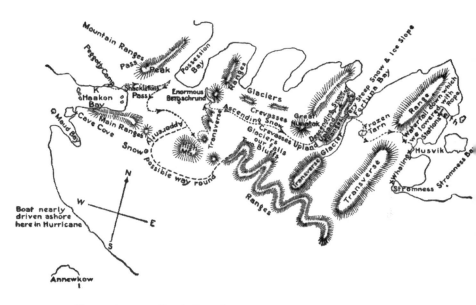

The route across South Georgia

decided to take a chance. They coiled the rope, all three sat on it in tandem fashion, arms around each other. In this manner they launched themselves into space, glissading down a long snow slope into unknown darkness, finishing up in a snowdrift, luckily unharmed. They had hurtled down 900 feet in a few minutes. Surviving many near-disasters they traversed two snowfields, four glaciers and three mountain ranges. They covered 40 miles in 36 hours, with only short rests for food. They dared not sleep. That journey was an epic on its own. Forty years later a party of experienced and well-equipped mountaineers repeated the climb by roughly the same route. Afterwards, their leader, Malcolm Burley, said: 'I don't know how they did it, except that they had to – three men of the heroic age of Antarctic exploration.'

Shackleton described their arrival at Stromness: 'Our logbook, cooker and adze were all that we brought out of the Antarctic, which we entered a year and a half before with a well-found ship, full equipment and high hopes. Our beards

The Shackleton Gap above King Haakon Bay

An uncouth trio approaches Stromness

were long and our hair matted. We were unwashed and the garments that we had worn for nearly a year without a change were tattered and stained. We smelled. Three more unpleasant-looking ruffians could hardly have been imagined.

'Down we hurried and when quite close to the station, we met two small boys[15] of ten or twelve years of age. I asked these lads where the manager's house was situated. They did not answer. They gave one look ... and ran from us as fast as their legs would carry them.'

Worsley, as usual, gives a graphic account of what happened next: 'We went on to Sorlee's house [Mr Sørlle was the local manager] and met a foreman. He said "What do

The South Ridge

The building formerly thought to be the manager's villa

you want?" Shackleton said "I want to see him, I know him."
The man went inside and told Sorlee: "There are three funny-
looking men outside, they say they know you." Sorlee came
out and Shackleton said: "Do you know me Sorlee?" Sorlee

Anne Marie Sørlle, possibly one of the 'boys' who ran away

Mr Sørlle (front), manager at Stromness. Frank Worsley (in uniform) is behind him

said "No". Then I said: "Do you know me?" He looked at me and said emphatically "No".'

When he grasped who they were his hospitality knew no bounds.

The story goes that an old Norwegian whaler, who was present, gave his own version of the meeting, in his broken English: 'Everbody know Shackleton well, and we very sorry he is lost in ice with all hands. We not know three terrible-looking bearded men who walk into office off the mountainside. Manager say "Who the hell are you?" And terrible bearded man in

The mountainous interior of South Georgia

'My name is Shackleton'

the centre of the three say, very quietly: "My name is Shackleton." Me, I turn aside and weep. I think manager weep too.'

Worsley describes a reception held for them: 'We went into a large, low room, full of captains and mates and sailors. Three or four white-haired veterans of the sea came forward; one spoke in Norse and the manager translated. He said he had been at sea over forty years; that he knew this stormy Southern Ocean, from South

George Herelle, then a Boy Scout at Port Stanley, when McCarthy, McNeish and Vincent arrived from South Georgia, helped to carry two who were badly frost-bitten to the hospital and was thanked by Shackleton

Captain Thom who captained the *Southern Sky* on Shackleton's first attempt to reach Elephant Island.

Georgia to Cape Horn, and never had he heard of such a wonderful feat of daring seamanship as bringing the 22 foot open boat from Elephant Island to South Georgia. He felt it an honour to meet and shake hands with Sir Ernest and his companions. He finished with a dramatic gesture: "These are men!"'

8

RESCUE FROM ELEPHANT ISLAND

Shackleton's first thoughts were for the men in King Haakon Bay. Their Norwegian host arranged immediately for a steam whaler to sail at once, and Worsley went with it to act as guide. Although a south-east gale blew all night, he slept between clean sheets for eleven hours. Worsley wrote: 'I awoke to find we were approaching the entrance to King Haakon Sound. Soon after, we passed our Cape Cove and Albatross Plateau. A blast from the whistle brought our men crawling out hastily ... We were ashore in three minutes ... we all ran the *James Caird* down to the beach, launched her and soon had her and them on board, steaming back full speed for Stromness. They landed the *James Caird* at Leith next day. The Norwegians (who insisted that the boat be brought back), would not let us put a hand to her, and every man in the place claimed the honour of helping to haul her up to the wharf. I think Shackleton must have thought it one of the proudest moments. The amazed admiration of these descendants of Vikings was so spontaneous and hearty it was quite affecting.'

Shackleton noted that a heavy snowstorm started two hours after the three reached the whaling station and by the

Shackleton (second from left) at Port Stanley, in the Falkland Islands. He cabled news of his survival and requested a rescue ship.

following morning deep snow lay everywhere. As soon as he had sent Worsley on his way to King Haakon Bay, he started planning the rescue of his twenty-two men on Elephant Island. His first attempt was made in the local whaler *Southern Sky*, which was at once placed at his disposal under an old friend, Captain Thom. But the pack ice barred their path 70 miles from Elephant Island. After several attempts to break through, they ran short of coal and he decided to visit Port Stanley in the Falkland Islands. He found no suitable ship there but was able to cable to England with news of his survival. He then contacted the authorities in Uruguay, who sent a trawler, the *Instituto de Pesca No 1*, which also failed to penetrate the pack ice. In July, in desperation, he took ship to Punta Arenas in the Straits of Magellan, where the British colony rallied round and

The *Yelcho* to the rescue

chartered the wooden schooner *Emma* for him. But once again the ring of ice forced him to return to Port Stanley, unsuccessful.

Finally, he returned to Punta Arenas where the Chilean government loaned him the steam tug *Yelcho*. She sailed with Shackleton, Worsley and Crean and a crew of Chilean Navy volunteers captained by Lieutenant Luis Pardo. On this fourth attempt they found a gap in the pack ice, located the camp and, on 30 August, found the twenty-two men alive and well, though exhausted and near starvation.

9

SURVIVAL ON
ELEPHANT ISLAND

rank Hurley, the expedition photographer, who, with Shackleton's agreement, had preserved over a hundred of his glass negatives and a quantity of cinematograph film, gives some idea[16] of what they went through while waiting to be rescued: 'Those first few days on Elephant Island were Hell, and it appeared at first as though many who had endured so far, would be unable to survive further persecution and exposure. Our new refuge was named Cape Wild – at once an apt description and a tribute to a great-hearted comrade. It was a spit of rock thrust out into the sea – with a sheer icecliff on the land side and a cluster of huge boulders just off its tip. The island coast curved towards it on one side, and formed the bay into which we had run and found our landing place.

'We re-rigged our tent and all hands turned to in the erection of a wind shelter for the cook's galley ... Weather conditions being still wretched, we retired daily at five o'clock to saturated sleeping-bags, to steam and fug for fourteen hours. The tent walls, becoming thickly covered with condensation rime, showered us with every gust.

'Here we were, a party of twenty-two, maintaining a precarious foothold on an exposed ledge of barren rock, in the world's wildest ocean ... Of our party, one was a helpless cripple, a dozen were more or less disabled with frostbite, and some were for the moment crazed with their privations. Our refuge was like the scrimped courtyard of a prison – a narrow strip of beach 200 paces long by 30 yards wide. Before us, the sea, which pounded our shores in heavy tumult, would at night be frozen into icy silence, only to break up again under tidal influence with a noise like the churning of some monstrous mill. Behind us the island peaks rose 3,000 feet into the air, and down their riven valleys across their creeping glaciers, the wind devils raced and

Left: The party marooned on Elephant Island

Preparing a camp

Digging in

shrieked, lashed us with hail and smothered us with snowdrift. Inhospitable, desolate and hemmed in with glaciers, our refuge was as uninviting as it well could be. Still, we were grateful. It was better than the ice-floes.

'On August 30th, the one hundred and thirty seventh day of our maroonment, Marston and I were scanning the northern horizon, when I drew his attention to a long, curious-shaped berg ... We continued to gaze at it when, miracle of miracles, a vessel came in sight from under its lee. We immediately raised a cry ... which was greeted by derision and mocking shouts. When at last we made them realise the truth, they came crawling through the roof and breaking through the walls [of the boat-hut]. Wild gave the

The men on Elephant Island sight the rescue ship

The end after four and a half months

Shackleton rescues his men

order to kindle the beacon. It was a worthy occasion on which to expend one of my three remaining spaces of film and it recorded faithfully that truly historic scene.

'Ringing cheers greeted its [the boat's] approach. Those on board returned our salvoes. Cheer followed cheer, the mountains cheered back.'

Shackleton, on board the *Yelcho*, had been searching the coastline of Elephant Island when Worsley recognised the camp. The Boss took a boat close in and describes the scene: 'There was no time then to exchange news or congratulations. I did not even go up the beach to inspect the camp. ... A heavy sea was running and a change of wind might bring the ice back at any time. I hurried the party aboard with all possible speed, taking the records of the Expedition.'

Thanks to the efforts of Frank Wild, their morale had remained high. They sailed within the hour lest the gap in

Yelcho returns in triumph

the ice should close. At Punta Arenas the whole town turned out to welcome them back to civilisation. Shackleton's final task was to travel via San Francisco and New Zealand, to the base on the Ross Sea, to pick up the support party awaiting his arrival from the opposite side of the continent. He had already heard, during his visit to the Falklands, that many difficulties had arisen there while he was stranded on the ice floes.

The survivors greeted at Punta Arenas

The local people welcome Shackleton's men

Hubert Hudson's sextant, loaned for the Boat Journey

When the *Yelcho* returned, Shackleton went to Santiago to thank President Juan Luis Fuentes for Chile's part in the rescue. Amongst the crew who went with him, thirteen signed the dinner menu. The signatures are (from top): Sir Ernest Shackleton, Frank Worsley (captain of *Endurance*), Leonard Hussey, Reginald James, George Marston, Thomas Orde-Lees, Lewis Rickinson, Alexander Kerr, Frank Wild, Dr James McIlroy, Tom Crean, Dr Alexander Macklin and Lionel Greenstreet.

It was not until the spring of 1917 that Shackleton was able to return to war-weary England. Almost at once, the government sent him back to South America, on a mission to help counteract German influence there, which was strong. With his own reputation at its peak, following his remarkable adventures in Antarctica, he acted as a notable ambassador.

Following that visit, he was put into Army uniform as Major Shackleton and sent, with Worsley, to the North Russian front to organise food and winter equipment for the British forces fighting there in semi-Arctic conditions.

10

THE *JAMES CAIRD* RETURNS TO ENGLAND

*T*he *James Caird* was eventually brought back to Birkenhead[17] in 1919, although details are sketchy. In December of that year Worsley and Stenhouse, who had been captain of Shackleton's second ship, *Aurora*, had the *Caird* put on an open railway wagon at Liverpool and escorted her to London. Worsley writes that Shackleton loaned her to the Middlesex Hospital and the medical

The *James Caird* in the Middlesex Hospital garden

The *James Caird* en route
to the Royal Albert Hall

students conveyed her through the streets, collecting money
for the hospital appeal fund. By then, of course, she was no
longer the boat that had survived the 800-mile voyage. In
King Haakon Bay, it will be recalled, her masts had been
unstepped and the decking, the two top strakes and the half-
deck aft, were all removed to lighten her, as the six survivors
were too weak to haul her over the boulders to safety, above
tide mark. A heavy sea had washed away her rudder,
although, by some odd trick of the tide, it floated back some
time later.

Shackleton gave a public lecture in the Royal Albert Hall,
in South Kensington, on 19 December, and showed the film
and slides of the expedition which Frank Hurley, the
expedition photographer, had brought back. Because of their
weight and bulk – they were glass plate negatives, stored in
tins – he had been allowed to bring only 150 of the best –
preserving them with great care during the voyage to
Elephant Island and for the four months which the party
spent marooned there. The *James Caird* was brought from
the Middlesex Hospital gardens, where she had been used to
collect money for the hospital appeal fund, and driven to the
Hall on an open lorry, arriving at the last moment.
Shackleton wanted to have her on the platform with him but
unfortunately she was too wide to pass through the doors,
so she had to be left outside.

The next appearance of the *James Caird* was on the roof of Selfridges department store in Oxford Street, near the Marble Arch. No enemy to publicity, Shackleton was on hand with Worsley, to see his boat swayed up the front of the building from the street and be photographed for the newspapers. That was on 14 February 1920. Shackleton's

Top: Shackleton watches as the *James Caird* is hoisted onto the roof garden at Selfridges

Left: Shackleton and Worsley watch the operation

The *James Caird* on Selfridges' roof. The small boy in the sailor suit supplied the photograph.

sister, Eleanor, told the Fishers, Shackleton's biographers, that an 'elderly man insisted on being allowed to get into the boat, explaining that he greatly admired Shackleton, to whose parents he had been supplying fish for 28 years; he had come up from Sydenham, in South London, where Shackleton had lived as a boy, especially to see the boat.'

According to Worsley, Shackleton then gave the *Caird* to John Quiller Rowett, a friend from his school days at

John Quiller Rowett

Dulwich College. A chance meeting in the street had brought them together again in 1920, at a time when Shackleton had begun to think about a new expedition and found that Rowett might be willing to help with financing it.

Out of this association grew the 'Shackleton-Rowett Oceanographical and Antarctic Expedition'. Rowett, it is said, had made a fortune from 'cornering' rum, and went on to become a well-known

134

breeder and exhibitor of pedigree livestock, which he kept on his 10,000-acre estate. A generous benefactor of the Middlesex Hospital, which explains Shackleton's connection with it, he also founded and endowed the Rowett Agricultural Research Institute in Aberdeen, which has, for many years, been the leading institution of its kind in the world. So, in 1921, the *James Caird* was moved to Ely Place, Rowett's country seat at Frant, near Tunbridge Wells.

Shackleton announced the plans for his new expedition at the end of June 1921 and towards the end of July, Rowett arranged a party for Sir Ernest and Lady Shackleton and the principal members of the expedition, at Ely Place. The Shackletons' son Eddie and their daughter, Cecily, were also invited. The opportunity for press publicity was not overlooked and a long and detailed description of the occasion appeared in the *Tunbridge Wells Advertiser*. The issue of 29 July includes this description of the *James Caird*: 'Sir Ernest pointed out to our representative the boat in which he made the 800 mile journey across the ice fields and Southern seas on his last expedition. The boat is lying in the park at Ely Place – a silent testimony to the pluck and endurance of men of British blood. It is a small, open, carvel-built boat, about 25 ft long, with a raised forecastle, and bears many scars and knocks. On the starboard bow is a patch crushed in by ice and temporarily repaired. On the port side, part of the wood-work has been splintered by being on the rocks. Rough timber has been used for strengthening the sails which were frozen stiff by the cold. The boat contains no tanks, and the only gear left in it – the actual gear, used by the rescue party on the journey to South Georgia – is made up of two masts and one oar. The name '*J. Caird*' is painted on the bow, (named after Sir *James Caird*). Skids for hauling the boat over the ice are still there.'

There are several interesting points in this description. In the first place, the patch on the starboard bow could have been the one remarked on by Worsley as the three boats approached Elephant Island. The carpenter must have repaired this when he decked her, before the boat set out for South Georgia, although there is such a hole visible in a photograph of the boat when she was displayed at the National Maritime Museum. Secondly, the reporter identified the boat as being 'carvel-built', not 'clinker-built', as Worsley described her erroneously in his second book. Thirdly, the splintered woodwork seen on the port side could have been acquired in King Haakon Bay, at the end of the voyage. Fourthly, the reference to 'rough timber used for strengthening the sails' is hardly credible. Perhaps the reporter misunderstood some off-the-cuff remark by Shackleton – about the frozen sails being 'stiff as a board', a not unusual description in sailing terms. There are neither masts nor sails to be seen in a photograph reproduced in the newspaper but old sails were found in the bottom of the boat later on. Lastly, 'tanks' would refer to the buoyancy tanks normally fitted in lifeboats. These appear to have been removed on Elephant Island to make more room for stores and ballast and enable the crew to crawl under the decking to the sleeping bags in the bow.

11

SHACKLETON'S LAST VOYAGE

*I*n September 1921 Shackleton sailed in the *Quest* on his last expedition, to carry out an elaborate scientific programme and, in the process, to circumnavigate the Antarctic continent. Rowett financed the expedition with a gift of £70,000 – about £1.5 million at today's value – while Sir Frederick Becker, a paper manufacturer, also contributed a considerable sum.

The *Quest* in the Pool of London

Once again, fate intervened. It is clear that Shackleton had always suspected that he suffered from a heart condition and, as a consequence, would never allow any of the expedition medical men to examine him. He undoubtedly had a very strong constitution, but had subjected it to extreme stresses in the course of his expeditions. At Rio de Janeiro, on his way south, he suffered a severe heart attack, although he managed to pass it off as something else. The expedition doctor, Alexander Macklin, who had served under him in the *Endurance*, was not taken in. Just after their arrival at Grytviken, in South Georgia, Shackleton had another attack on board the *Quest*, followed almost immediately by a massive coronary thrombosis, from which he died. It was 5 January 1922 – only five weeks short of his forty-eighth birthday.

His body was taken to Montevideo, where it was given a remarkable reception by the people of Uruguay. Their President issued a most extraordinary eulogy:

Sir Ernest Shackleton synthesised every splendid quality; courage, always quiet and modest; limitless abnegation; fine tenacity ... all applied to the conquest of universal science, with a life-long devotion. Explorer of unknown regions, a famous geographer, interested in everything that tends to give a man a full knowledge of this planet on which he lives. Shackleton is not only one of the great glories of England, but is also a magnificent type of humanity. In an age of war-like heroism, he was the hero, calm and strong, who left behind him neither death nor grief.

An entry in the 1922 issue of the *Dulwich Year Book* produced for former pupils of Shackleton's old school, includes the eulogy quoted above and goes on to explain the circumstances of his burial:

A last farewell from Shackleton

SIR ERNEST SHACKLETON

It was originally proposed that Sir Ernest Shackleton's body should be brought home for burial, but Lady Shackleton decided, in deference to what, it is believed, would have been the explorer's own wish, that it should be taken back from Montevideo to South Georgia and interred on the island. Therefore, on February 15th – the 48th anniversary of his birth – with state ceremonial, the body was conveyed on a gun-carriage through the troop-lined streets of Montevideo and placed in the British whaler *Woodville*, which took the dead explorer on his last voyage south. A magnificent bronze wreath was sent by the Uruguayan Government, and wreaths from relatives and Mr J Q Rowett (OA),[18] who was mainly responsible for financing the *Quest* Expedition. A bronze memorial statue presented by the Old Alleynians in Montevideo and Buenos Ayres, a bronze wreath from the English community in Montevideo, and many others filled the carriage. The Uruguayan Government generously offered to transport the remains in a warship but owing to conditions in the South Atlantic this was not feasible. The cruiser *Uruguay*, however, escorted the *Woodville* to the limit of territorial waters, and before leaving, fired a salute of 19 guns, then, steaming abreast, the marines lined up at the salute. Bugles sounded the 'Farewell', and the cruiser dipped her ensign, and turned and steamed home.

The burial took place on 1 March, at the English church at Grytyiken [*sic*], South Georgia – 'the gate of the Antarctic' – the scene of his great exploit in 1916, when he reached the island in his journey to bring relief to the men of the lost *Endeavour*[19] and the scene of his death on 5th January. He lies buried in the everlasting snows.

Top: Shackleton's
cortège at
Montevideo

Left: Dr Alex
Macklin, who
attended his friend
Shackleton at his
death

Shackleton would surely have appreciated, in his own way, the 'pomp and circumstance' of his send-off from Uruguay, a gesture almost regal in its content and generous to a degree from a nation that was not his own. He was actually buried in the Norwegian cemetery at Grytviken, his resting place surrounded by graves of whalers who had preceded him, a choice that would, without doubt, have appealed to him. The original wooden cross was replaced in 1928 by a formal granite headstone and kerb, brought from England, bearing this simple inscription on the face:

Ernest Henry Shackleton
Explorer
Born 15th Feb. 1874
Entered Life Eternal
5th Jan. 1922

This is surmounted by his talisman, a nine-pointed star. On the reverse is a quotation from Browning, his favourite poet:

I hold that a man should strive to the uttermost for his life's set prize.

On the headland above the little town, a large cross has since been erected in his memory. Whalers adopted the habit of giving a ceremonial 'hoot' on their ship's sirens as they sailed by.[20]

On 2 March 1922, a memorial service for Sir Ernest Shackleton was held in St Paul's Cathedral in London, attended by representatives of the King, the Dowager Queen Alexandra, his family, the Alleyn Club and many dignitaries and friends.

A memorial was erected in London by the Royal Geographical Society. Designed by Sir Edwin Lutyens, the most distinguished architect of his time, it consists of a statue by

Shackleton's coffin in the chapel at Grytviken

Shackleton is buried among the whalers at Grytviken

143

Top: The cross on the headland above Grytviken

Left: A granite headstone replaced the original wooden cross in 1928

A cairn and cross erected near Grytviken

A statue of Shackleton by Charles Jagger to a design by Sir Edwin Lutyens stands outside the Royal Geographical Society in London

the sculptor Charles Jagger, showing the explorer clad in Antarctic garb. It was erected in 1932, in a niche in the outer wall of the Society's building in Kensington, facing onto Exhibition Road.

Acknowledged as one of the greatest Antarctic explorers of all time, Shackleton's epic open-boat journey will surely live for ever as the greatest survival story in the history of polar exploration. To have brought every member of the *Endurance* party home safely, in the face of such incredible hardships, first on the ice floes, then in the three boats to Elephant Island, was a feat of supreme leadership. The 800-mile journey in an open boat, the climb over the mountains of South Georgia, and finally, the rescue of the twenty-two men from Elephant Island, at the fourth attempt, might almost be seen as acts of faith.

Shackleton's name has been given to many landmarks in the Antarctic and even further afield. Sir Vivian Fuchs named his Weddell Sea base after him in 1958, as well as the Shackleton range of mountains which he encountered when his party crossed the Antarctic continent by the route Shackleton had planned to follow when fate stepped in to frustrate him. There is also a Shackleton Glacier, a Shackleton Coast, a Shackleton Inlet, a Shackleton Icefall and a Shackleton Ice Shelf. Above King Haakon Bay in South Georgia, where he broke through the mountain range, during his crossing of the island, is the Shackleton Gap. More recently, the Royal Air Force named a long-range reconnaissance aircraft the 'Shackleton', and his memory

The RAF Shackleton reconnaissance aircraft

The British Post Office issued a postage stamp in Shackleton's honour in 1973

was honoured in a special issue of British Polar stamps.

In August 1994 his fame took extraterrestrial flight when the crater on the moon nearest to its South Pole was named Shackleton Crater at the General Assembly of the Inter-national Astronomical Union, at The Hague.

Perhaps the most notable tribute to Shackleton, among many, was written by Sir Raymond Priestley, a member of the *Nimrod* expedition in 1907–09:

> For scientific leadership, give me Scott, for swift and efficient travel, Amundsen. But when you are in a hopeless situation, when you are seeing no way out, get down on your knees and pray for Shackleton. Incomparable in adversity, he was the miracle worker who would save your life against all the odds and long after your number was up. The greatest leader that ever came on God's earth, bar none.

12

FROM DULWICH
TO GREENWICH
AND BACK

*T*he story of the *James Caird* changed course completely when her sea-going days came to an end. A mere eight years old, several lifetimes of experience had been crammed into that short existence. A boat at sea is a living thing – her timbers move and creak and the wind whistles tunes through the spars and rigging. Ashore and divorced from her native element, a boat loses this quality, and so might it have been with the *James Caird*, but for the name of Shackleton and the famous voyage.

Built in 1914 in an Isle of Dogs boatyard, she had survived rebuilding and man-haulage over the ice, more reconstruction on Elephant Island, a seventeen-day voyage through the Southern Ocean, near-disembowelling on South Georgia, repeated dragging over boulders there and upending to form Peggotty Camp, transportation to Grytviken in 1916, a 7,000-mile voyage by ship to Birkenhead and thence by train to London in 1919, use as an open-air exhibit at the Middlesex Hospital, hauling up onto the roof of Selfridges department store for publicity, and then transport to a private estate at Frant in Sussex. Later on she was moved to Dulwich College as a memorial to Shackleton where she survived a bomb blast and suffered a period of neglect, followed by a move to Greenwich and reconstruction, a period of cramped discomfort, still unrigged until she finally returned to Dulwich College. There she rose like a phoenix from the ashes, fully rigged and displayed as a fitting memorial to a great leader.

The only artifact of any size to survive from the well-found but ill-fated *Endurance* expedition, which sailed into the Antarctic in 1914, the *James Caird* inevitably became the focus of the Shackleton legend. A few other items survive, the chief being Frank Hurley's collection of remarkable photographs and his film of the *Endurance* expedition. Queen Alexandra's Bible survives[21] and so do the log and the sextant used on the boat journey. Hussey's banjo and a few documents, a couple of sledges, a sweater, a blanket and a 'helmet' remain from other expeditions, while in New Zealand an Arrol–Johnston car and a Primus are preserved. The Antarctic Heritage Trust in New Zealand also has the care of Shackleton's hut at Cape Royds in McMurdo Sound.

One nevertheless gets the impression that Shackleton lost interest in his boat when she had served her purpose. In his book *South*, his saga of the expedition, he tells how the Norwegians insisted on bringing her back from King Haakon Bay, but that is the last time that he mentioned her. In South Georgia, all his energy was directed towards the rescue of his twenty-two companions marooned on Elephant Island. The fate of his men was everything to him and he does not seem to have been greatly bothered about the fate of his boat.

On the other hand, the Norwegian whalers regarded that battered hulk almost as a sacred relic, many seeking the honour of helping to haul her ashore. However, when the *Caird* reached London in 1919, Shackleton found her useful for publicity purposes to help drum up interest in his lectures.

It must be remembered that a mere twelve months had passed since the horrors of the Great War had ended and many still wondered what on earth Shackleton and his men had been doing down in the South, instead of fighting for King and Country. Nevertheless, he still had to raise funds by every possible means to pay off the debts of the expedition.

The photograph of the *James Caird* at the Middlesex Hospital shows a craft similar to many others hauled up on the beaches of seaside towns and fishing villages around the coasts of Britain. Her decrepit state prompts the question – did Shackleton explain to his audiences that she had looked somewhat different during her 800-mile voyage? To the initiated, it was obvious that, in her stripped-down form, she could not possibly have survived it, but what of the uninitiated majority, ignorant of the ways of the sea? Did they grasp it? Is it possible that Shackleton, who was a bit of a joker, did not bother to disabuse them? Later on, when the boat was displayed at Dulwich College in the same state, without masts, sails and decking, the unspoken assumption must have been that this was her condition during the famous voyage.

Dulwich College, Shackleton's old school, was the first institution to have the care of the *James Caird*. Like most of England's public schools, Dulwich College has an ancient pedigree. It was founded in 1619 by Edward Alleyn, who achieved fame as an actor-manager in the time of Shakespeare. As part-owner of the Rose Theatre in Southwark and later of the Fortune Theatre, and appointed 'Master of the Royal Game of Bears, Bulls and Mastiff Dogs' to King James I and VI, he grew wealthy, bought the manor of Dulwich in the county of Surrey and there founded the College of God's Gift to provide for the education of 'six poor Brethren, six poor Sisters, and twelve poor Scholars'. In 1842 the College became a grammar school to extend its intake of pupils for the benefit of the locality. An Act of

Parliament in 1857 revised completely the terms of the foundation and the College was developed on its present site in the style which it retains to this day, providing now for the education of more than 1,400 boys, drawing upon an even wider area in South London. In the main, it is a day school, but with some 100 boarders.

In March 1922, the Alleyn Club, members of which are former pupils of Dulwich College, opened an appeal fund for a Shackleton Memorial, whereupon John Quiller Rowett OA, to whom Shackleton had given the *James Caird*, presented it to his old school and the gift was accepted gratefully as an appropriate memorial to the explorer.

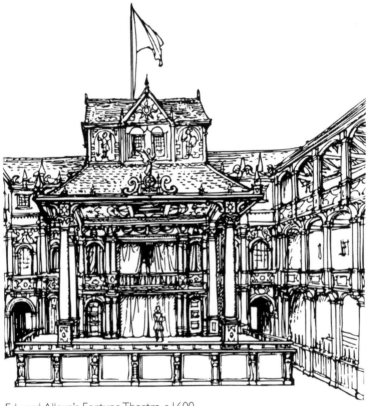

Edward Alleyn's Fortune Theatre c.1600

Dulwich College, painted by Camille Pissarro in 1870

The *James Caird* at Dulwich College, 1924–67

A special shelter was designed to house it, adjoining the School's Swimming Bath block, at a cost of £369. The Alleyn Club contributed £200, already collected, for ornamental railings to surround the display.

The *James Caird* was delivered to Dulwich on 11 April 1924 and was placed in her new home with appropriate ceremony. A year later a bronze tablet was prepared, measuring 19 inches by 14 inches, with the following inscription:

THE SHACKLETON MEMORIAL

In this boat, Shackleton, with five comrades, made in 1916 his famous voyage of 800 miles of Antarctic sea to South Georgia. This voyage resulted in his saving the lives of the 22 members of the Endurance Expedition, who were marooned on Elephant Island.

To recall his heroism to the boys of Dulwich, the Boat was presented to the College by Dr. J.Q. Rowett O.A.

Sir Ernest Henry Shackleton Born February 15th 1874. Entered Dulwich College May 1887. Left April 1890. Died January 5th, 1922 on board the 'Quest'. Buried at Grytyiken, South Georgia.[22]

Detur Gloria Soli Deo

In retrospect, the position chosen for the memorial was strangely off the beaten track for such an important possession. It was remote from the main centre of school activities and one came across it almost by accident. For the next twenty years the *James Caird* enjoyed a tranquil

The *James Caird* during the 1930s

The *James Caird* loaned for the British Polar Exhibition, 1930

existence, except for a short interlude in July 1930 when she was loaned to the British Polar Exhibition, staged at the Central Hall, Westminster. A sledge used by Shackleton for his attempt on the South Pole in 1908–09, which had been given to the College in 1924, was also on display. The event and the details of the open-boat journey were recorded in the *Geographical Journal,* the periodical of the Royal Geographical Society.[23] In 1942 the mayor of the South London borough of Lambeth asked to borrow the boat to exhibit in a 'war weapons week' in March of that year. Any association with war weapons seems odd, considering that the *James Caird* had spent the 1914–18 war in the Antarctic, battling with the forces of nature. The Governors of the College turned down the request 'in view of the fragile nature of the boat'.

The 'fragile' *James Caird* nevertheless stood up well to her next trial. Towards the end of the Second World War the enemy resorted to two types of 'V' or revenge weapons, with which they bombarded London and south-east England. The V2, a long-range rocket, was slightly less alarming than the V1, because the sound of its approach was only audible after it had exploded. The V1 was a flying bomb, similar to a pilotless aircraft, which 'motored' with a distinctive and ominous roar at a relatively low altitude. If the sound of the approaching motor cut out overhead, one dived for cover. The V1 carried a bomb that exploded on impact and those that penetrated the defences of urban areas caused a great deal of destruction from blast.

On 25 July 1944 a V1 exploded in the College grounds with devastating effect. The architect to the College reported later that:

A flying bomb (V1) fell in the gravelway between the Science Block and the group of buildings comprising the Armoury, Squash and Fives Courts. The violence of the high explosive charge destroyed some of the nearby buildings, seriously damaged others, and caused damage to all the more distant buildings. One half of the large Science Block has been destroyed, the Boiler House, Gymnasium and Engineering Block have also been

Bomb damage at
Dulwich College
in 1944

The wrecked Science block

damaged to a lesser degree. The Swimming Bath roof has
collapsed. This has happened on 10th July 1944,
fortunately at 10 o'clock in the evening so that no-one was
injured. The devastation was widespread indeed, but the
James Caird survived unscathed.

In 1958 a publicity agent in the United States sought to
borrow the boat to publicise a book about the famous boat
journey. He presumed it was 'gathering dust in the basement
of some museum or institution in London'. When located, he
hoped that some shipping line would be glad to transport her
gratis to New York 'for the publicity'. A source in London
replied that, far from being 'stuck in some basement', the
James Caird was the valued possession of Dulwich College,
Shackleton's old school, and doubted whether the authorities
would lend her because of the risk of damage in transit. In
the event, the College was never approached and nothing
more was heard of the proposal.

Twenty-three years after the bombing the *James Caird* was still in her original shelter, but new buildings were being planned for that area and the boat had perforce to be moved. In January 1967 a new Master (headmaster) of the College, David Emms, was appointed, who was also a Trustee of the National Maritime Museum at Greenwich. He noted with concern that the *James Caird*, in her delapidated surroundings, had tended to become a receptacle for unwanted rubbish. Some oars, spars and sails, and the sledge mentioned above, lay in the bottom of the boat, neglected and in a very poor state. As something had clearly to be done to preserve this important possession she was offered, on temporary loan, to the National Maritime Museum and in due course the offer was accepted. When construction of the Composite Block, planned for the devastated area, was about to begin, the *James Caird* was moved to Greenwich.

The National Maritime Museum forms part of a large and very fine complex of buildings associated with seafaring and navigation situated on the south bank of the River Thames in the Royal Park of Greenwich, downstream from the Tower of London. A royal palace was built there in the time of King Henry V and the site has since been used by various monarchs as a royal abode. The oldest building still standing is the Queen's House, an architectural gem, designed by Inigo Jones in 1616 for Anne of Denmark, spouse of James I and VI. It was followed by two buildings designed by Sir Christopher Wren: the Royal Observatory, commissioned in 1675, and built on an eminence in the middle of Greenwich Park overlooking the other, the Royal Naval College. Originally the Hospital for Seamen, the latter was begun about the same time and added to later by Wren's assistant Nicholas Hawksmoor and by Sir John Vanbrugh. The buildings used for the Museum are the work of several nineteenth-century designers, the blocks being linked on either side of the Queen's House by colonnades, erected in

Top: The National Maritime Museum at Greenwich with the Queen's House by Inigo Jones in the centre and Wren's Royal Hospital, later the Royal Naval College, where Frank Worsley subsequently lectured, beyond

Left: The *James Caird* unrigged at Greenwich in 1967

1809 as a memorial to Nelson, who had died at Trafalgar four years previously.

The National Maritime Museum was established by Act of Parliament in 1934 for the study of maritime history and to house several collections of ship models, manuscripts, paintings and memorabilia relating to the sea. The main collection was assembled by another Sir James Caird, a wealthy Dundee shipowner. Curiously, he was from the same city, but no relation of the man who sponsored Shackleton's expedition. The Museum at Greenwich is now the leading institution of its kind in the world.

At first, the *Caird* joined the Tristan da Cunha longboat and similar craft, outside the Neptune Hall, but two months later she was placed inside the Hall, resting on chocks and with the mainmast stepped. She remained there on display until it was decided, in the summer of 1968, to restore her to the state she was in when she made her historic voyage. She was taken to Cory's Barge Works at Charlton nearby, where a shipwright repaired the hull, replaced the two strakes which had been removed in King Haakon Bay, supplied masts, yards and a boom for the mizzen mast, and a rudder. She was given a solid timber deck in place of the original canvas one and, by good fortune, a bolt of old Navy canvas was found, sufficient to supply a suit of sails. By September 1968, the *James Caird* was back in the Neptune Hall, rigged as a ketch, with a jib and standing lugsails on main and mizzen masts. She had a curious hole in the bow on the port side, which no one seems able to explain.

In the meantime there seem to have been some misgivings at Dulwich. At a meeting of the Governors of the College in May 1968, the Clerk reminded the Board that the boat was on temporary loan to the Museum only while the new Composite Block was being built. It appeared, however, that no provision had been made for her in the designs for the new buildings. Where was she supposed to go? Should she

Top: A model of the *James Caird*

Left: The *James Caird* rigged at Greenwich in 1968

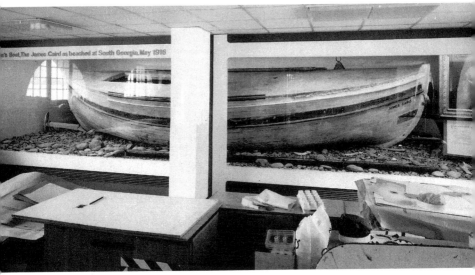

The *James Caird* in the Half-Deck at Greenwich

be left on permanent loan to the Museum? The Clerk then outlined the conditions on which the *James Caird* had been given to the College in 1922 and it was agreed unanimously that she should be returned to the College and the architect instructed to make provision for her.

Five months later the subject came up again. It was pointed out that the Museum had carried out considerable restoration work on the boat and that she had been rigged with masts and sails. She was therefore in fine condition but, unfortunately, because the height of the masts had not been allowed for in the new design, she could not be accommodated in the cloister of the new Dining Hall Block as intended, there being insufficient headroom. The Board then reversed its decision and agreed to offer the boat to the Museum on permanent loan. In return, the latter was asked to supply a scale model of the *James Caird* for display at the College. The Museum had a model made, as requested, fitted into a display case, and decorated with Hurley photographs.

In July 1970, this model was installed in the Lower Hall

Top and right:
The interior of
the *James Caird*

The *James Caird* stripped down at Greenwich

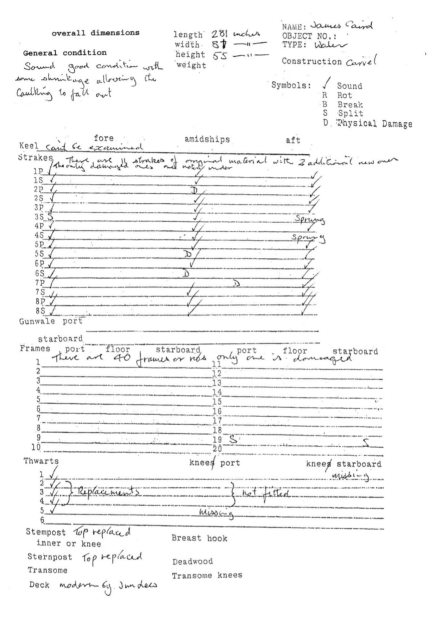

A survey of the *James Caird* undertaken by the National Maritime Museum, Greenwich

at Dulwich College. The model is fully rigged but, for some reason at the time of writing it has a gaff on the mizzen mast, unlike the full-size boat, which has a standing lugsail – believed to be the correct rig. The financial arrangement between the College and the Museum was in the nature of a swap. The College agreed to pay £250 for the model but, because it had earlier spent an equivalent sum on restoration work to the *Caird*, the Museum agreed to meet half that sum; thus in the end the College paid the Museum £125.

At the end of 1969 the Neptune Hall at the Maritime Museum had to be closed for reconstruction and the *James Caird* was unrigged and moved into the Museum's store at Kidbrooke, where she remained for the next four and a half years. Then, during 1970, it was proposed that she should become part of a new Polar Gallery to be established in the basement of the East Wing of the Museum, which would also include Arctic, Antarctic and whaling artifacts. All this would supplement an existing collection of Arctic exhibits on the ground floor. Unfortunately, this scheme had to be changed when it was realised that the electrical installation already occupied a large part of the basement and this would prevent the planned display from being connected physically with the existing one. The basement area eventually became a Children's or Junior Centre and was christened the Half-Deck. It was opened formally by Princess Anne in May 1974.

It was in the Half-Deck that the *James Caird* reappeared. Keeping to a directive from on high, the curator had to squeeze her into a display at the north end but, because the ceiling was too low, she was shown shorn of masts, sails and rigging. The well-arranged display included a portrait of Shackleton by Eves, which the Museum had acquired earlier, and an illustrated description of the famous voyage. An appropriate background touch was provided by a supply of grey boulders from Cape Rosa, the point at the entrance to King Haakon Bay where the *James Caird* first touched land

The late Lord Shackleton at his father's centenary celebration in the Queen's House at Greenwich in 1974 with his sister-in-law Mrs Brenda Shackleton and her son Richard Shackleton

on South Georgia in May 1916. These had been collected and shipped to the Museum by members of the British Antarctic Survey and added one more authentic touch to the display. In the event, the supply of stones was deemed insufficient, and after consulting the Museum geologist, a similar type of boulder was found to exist on the foreshore at Aberystwyth in Wales, and a truck-load was supplied from there by the Cyngor Dosbarth Ceredigion District Council.

The hundredth anniversary of Shackleton's birth fell on 15 February 1974. A gathering to celebrate it was held on 9 May of that year beside his boat in the Half-Deck, three months late because the gallery was not ready in February. A toast was drunk to the explorer's memory and later that

Former curator of the Polar Gallery, Ann Savours, now Mrs Shirley, at the Queen's House ceremony

evening a reception was held in the formal splendour of the Queen's House, attended by Lord Shackleton, son of Sir Ernest, and other members of his family, Sir Vivian Fuchs, who achieved the trans-Antarctic crossing forty years after Shackleton's ill-fated attempt, and others associated with the Antarctic, in celebration of the great explorer's achievements.

The *James Caird* had been put through a comprehensive survey by the Museum's conservation officer who reported that she was still 'sound, good condition with some shrinkage allowing the caulking to fall out'. Of her thirteen strakes, eleven were original, two had 'sprung' and two were the new replacements referred to earlier. Of her forty 'frames or ribs', only one was damaged. Of her five 'thwarts', two were missing. The tops had been replaced on her 'stempost' and her 'sternpost' but her keel was impossible to inspect. For a boat nearly seventy years old, which had experienced the onslaughts of Antarctic weather for months on end, being dragged over the ice floes and the foreshores of Elephant Island and South Georgia, as well as the blast of a V1 flying bomb, the report speaks well for the specifications of Frank Worsley and the construction by W. & J. Leslie and Co. In 1984, when the Lower Hall at Dulwich College was refurbished, the National Maritime Museum supplied a new showcase and display for the model of the *James Caird*, replacing the original one which was showing signs of wear and tear.

In March 1986 the Director of the Museum wrote to the Master of the College to explain that the East Wing would have to be closed for structural alterations and the Museum would no longer be able to display the boat. What should they do with it? This letter enclosed a copy of another, written to the editor of *The Scotsman* newspaper in Edinburgh the previous December by Commander Angus Erskine, a well-known Antarctic traveller and enthusiast. In this he welcomed the plan to move Captain Scott's first polar exploration ship, *Discovery*, from her berth in St Katherine's Dock on the Thames, to the new Heritage Museum in Dundee, where she was built, and went on to ask:

> Now will someone rescue Shackleton's 22 foot boat, the *James Caird*, in which he made his famous open-boat journey from Elephant Island to South Georgia in 1916? It lies today in a corner of the educational department of the National Maritime Museum, Greenwich, and members of the public have to ask special permission to see it. I suggest that it should be in a prominent position in the Royal Scottish Museum where it would be an inspiration to adventurous persons, young and old.

The letter went on to outline Shackleton's connections with Scotland, which were many. Commander Erskine undoubtedly had a point. If Greenwich had lost interest in displaying the *James Caird*, there were others who would be very glad to have the care of such a famous boat. And why not Scotland? Two Scots, Beardmore and Caird, had been the main sponsors for two of Shackleton's Antarctic expeditions. Shackleton had been Secretary of the Royal Scottish Geographical Society and had stood for Parliament, albeit unsuccessfully, in Caird's home city of Dundee. In addition, Sir James Caird had made the *Endurance* expedition possible. The *Discovery*, in which Shackleton had sailed as Third Officer under Captain Scott in 1901 was, in fact, moved from the Thames to Dundee five months after Erskine's letter was published. The Museum's indirect suggestion for the future of the *Caird* revived an idea that had been circulating at Greenwich as early as 1983.

At Dulwich this news was seen as the writing on the wall. It was acknowledged that the boat belonged to Dulwich College but the school had been content with the arrangements at Greenwich. Shackleton was undoubtedly a national figure and if his boat had been displayed there to the satisfaction of all concerned, that was indeed a logical place for her. The suggestion that she might be sent across the Border, however, made people sit up. The then Head of Library at Dulwich and custodian of the College archives, which include a precious collection of Shackleton records, immediately visited the National Maritime Museum and, with the authority of the Master of the College, made it quite clear that the *James Caird* should be returned to Dulwich. In the autumn of 1986, the East Wing at Greenwich was closed, a hole was knocked in the outer wall of the building as the only means of extracting the boat from the basement and, together with the boulders and two sledges formerly used by Shackleton, the *James Caird* was returned to Dulwich. On arrival there the boat and the sledges were consigned, for the time being, to the newly built groundsman's store. Still unrigged, looking rather small, forlorn and insignificant, much as she had when displayed in the Middlesex Hospital garden in 1919, she rested in a corner among the mowing machines.

A protracted discussion then ensued at Dulwich over a period of months. The problem was not an easy one. Was the College the appropriate place to house this famous boat? If displayed at the school, she should be accessible to members of the public, yet protected from the elements and possible vandalism. The cost might be considerable – should funds be diverted from educational purposes to display her properly? Should an appeal be made for funds? This had to be ruled out because another appeal was being planned already, to create bursaries. As an alternative, the possibility of offering her on loan to other institutions was considered.

Dundee was quickly rejected as being too far away. The Dulwich Picture Gallery, an ancient foundation and part of the Dulwich complex, did not consider her an appropriate exhibit. A College committee, sitting in March 1988, learned that neither the Chelsea Harbour Development nor the Museum of London wanted the boat, but that St Katherine's Dock, near the Tower of London, and the Chatham Historic Dockyard Museum were interested, the last very much so. However, a shadow loomed over these proceedings in the form of the Alleyn Club, with its membership of 6,000 former pupils of Dulwich College, who were believed to have a sentimental attachment to the *James Caird*. One thing was clear: the College was determined to retain ownership and any arrangement to display her somewhere else would only be on the basis of a loan, under strict conditions, in view of what had happened at Greenwich. In the summer of 1988 the Chairman at Chatham, Sir Steuart Pringle, visited the College to inspect the boat, which still remained in the groundsman's shed.

By then, however, opinion in favour of retaining the *James Caird* at Dulwich was hardening. When a costly scheme to

Lord Shackleton views the *James Caird* at Dulwich, 1989

display her, running into five figures, was proposed by a firm of architects, the College turned to the National Maritime Museum for advice. The Museum was most helpful, suggesting how the boat might be displayed and protected in the North Cloister of the College at a fraction of the cost of the first scheme.

The plans submitted by the Museum were agreed, contracts for the work were placed during the summer of 1989 and new flooring was laid during the summer vacation. On 30 August, small-boat specialists from the Ship Department of the Maritime Museum supervised the hauling of the *James Caird* from the groundsman's store to the North Cloister, inching her through the doorway with millimetres to spare on either side. She was then rigged by Museum staff,

The *James Caird* displayed at Dulwich College, 1990

with masts, stays, halliards, jib, mainsail and mizzen, and restored, as far as can be ascertained, to the state in which she made her famous voyage. Enclosed by a solid rail and supports in nautical style, resting on the boulders from South Georgia and Aberystwyth, with a well-arranged display of photographs and diagrams, she now looks very imposing and much larger than formerly, her mainmast just clearing the cloister ceiling. In a coat of white paint to set her off, with her name *James Caird* in black letters on her starboard bow, she is a worthy monument to the man who made that famous voyage in her.

On 12 September 1989 Lord Shackleton, son of the explorer and likewise well-versed in the affairs of the Antarctic, visited Dulwich College to open their new Shackleton classroom building and inspect the *James Caird* in her role as the school's memorial to his famous father.

13

THE JAMES CAIRD
SOCIETY

*I*n the autumn of 1993 the College received a request
from the organisers of the annual London International Boat Show. Would the College agree to lend
the *James Caird* for display as a special feature in the
Exhibition Hall at Earls Court, West London, for ten days in
January 1994? The event would coincide with the attempt
by Trevor Potts and three companions to repeat Sir Ernest
Shackleton's voyage in the *James Caird* from Elephant Island
to South Georgia, providing a topical reason for the presence
of the boat. Trevor Potts was leader of the *In the Wake of
Shackleton* expedition. He had had a replica of the *James
Caird* built and named *Sir Ernest Shackleton*, in order to
repeat the famous voyage – his boyhood ambition. This was
reaching its climax just as the exhibition was due to begin at
Earls Court.

The authorities at Dulwich agreed to the proposal, mainly
because it would enable the boat to be seen by a wider public
than was possible at Dulwich. In the event the results were
quite remarkable. One problem did arise – the high cost of
extracting the boat from its enclosure. The railings around it

had to be cut through and the doors and door frames to the cloister removed and replaced – four operations – in addition to the cost of transport and insurance. In the event a white knight in the shape of an anonymous donor came to the rescue and the *James Caird* was moved to Earls Court just before Christmas.

The position allotted was a prominent one near the main entrance. The display panels from Dulwich were re-erected on the stand, together with several enlargements of Hurley's photographs. The boat was fully rigged and the Dulwich video programme *Shackleton's Boat Journey* was displayed continuously on a VDU screen. One end of the stand was devoted to a display dealing with Trevor Potts' expedition.

The Boat Show opened on 5 January, incidentally the anniversary of Shackleton's death. Management of the *James Caird* display fell into the lap of the author as there was no one else to undertake it. To assist him, his son, two daughters, two granddaughters and various of their friends formed a rota, backed up with great enthusiasm by the late Lord Shackleton's daughter and a posse of Sea Cadets supplied by another enthusiast. They were kept busy throughout, running a competition, selling various items to help finance the *In the Wake of Shackleton* expedition and keeping track of the expedition's progress by means of satellite and fax communication.

The *James Caird*'s public debut had some very interesting results. Descendants of crew members of the *Endurance* expedition introduced themselves at the *James Caird* display, including those of Blackborow the stowaway, Marston the artist, Hussey the geologist, and relations of Shackleton himself. Some visitors were very knowledgeable about Shackleton and his expeditions, but in general the public's notions were lamentably vague and inaccurate. A minority knew that the boat was normally to be seen at Dulwich College, although the majority was unaware that she had

Lord Shackleton,
the explorer's
younger son

The *James Caird* at the London Boat Show in January 1994

Top: Trevor Potts' *Sir Ernest Shackleton*, his replica of the *James Caird*, off Elephant Island in December 1993

Right: The *Sir Ernest Shackleton* was ferried to Elephant Island

Top: The *Sir Ernest Shackleton* is lowered into the sea

Left: Trevor Potts

The *Caird* is taken out of the North Cloister   The *Caird* en route for the Boat Show

ever come back from Antarctica. All experience confirmed the wisdom of lending the *James Caird* for public exhibition.

Early on the very day – 5 January – that the exhibition opened, Trevor Potts in the *Sir Ernest Shackleton*, after a long struggle in a force 8 gale to avoid the perils of a lee shore, rounded the north-west corner of South Georgia, dropped anchor in the calm waters of Elsehul Bay and went to sleep. Meanwhile, at the Boat Show, interviewers from the BBC World Service stopped beside the *James Caird* and asked about the displays. Fortunately, Alexandra, Sir Ernest Shackleton's granddaughter, was on hand with the story of his ill-fated expedition and the epic of the *James Caird*. The details of Trevor Potts' voyage were provided by the author, who had, by chance, acted as Potts' unpaid press officer because earlier arrangements had fallen through.

In the middle of the afternoon the crew of the *Sir Ernest Shackleton* woke up and one of them switched on the radio and heard the announcement: 'This is the BBC World Service. We are now going over to the Boat Show at Earls Court.' They heard the interview, from several thousand miles away, verbatim from beside the actual *James Caird*. The contrast with Shackleton's landing on South Georgia could hardly have been greater.

With the *James Caird* safely back at Dulwich at the end of the Boat Show, those involved took stock. It was clear that

The author, assisted by his grandsons George, James and Alexander Woodrow

the universal interest shown by visitors to the *James Caird* display had to be followed up. During the months of March and April, the author sounded out the opinions of those who had helped at the Boat Show and among the authorities at Dulwich College, as to the possibility of forming a James Caird Society to ensure that the story of Shackleton's expeditions and the epic of his voyage in the *James Caird* should never be forgotten.

On 19 May 1994 the Master of the College welcomed a representative gathering of Shackleton enthusiasts to an inaugural meeting at Dulwich College to launch The James Caird Society. A group of founder members led by the late Lord Shackleton had already agreed, generously, to give their support in order to get the plan off the ground. The rapid growth of membership since has indicated that the Society is filling a real need. The success of its evening functions, held at Dulwich beside the *James Caird*, has proved their popularity. A joint lecture meeting held in December 1994 by the Royal Geographical Society in its lecture theatre, to hear Trevor Potts describe his expedition, was a welcome acknowledgement, only six months after its inauguration, of the Society's status.

Within a year of its formation, membership had passed the three figure mark. Not only has support come from within the United Kingdom but members have joined from overseas, from Australia, New Zealand, Canada, the United States and Norway, countries where the reputations of Shackleton and the *James Caird* are held in high regard. The James Caird Society continues to flourish, with membership approaching 600.

Celebrating the first birthday of The James Caird Society, (l–r) Harding Dunnett, Chairman; The Hon. Alexandra Shackleton, President and John Bardell, Vice Chairman

A chair from the manager's villa at Stromness in South Georgia, presented to Dulwich College by Noel Baker in 1962.

The James Caird Society original committee in session, 1995

APPENDICES

THE CONSTRUCTION OF THE
JAMES CAIRD

Clinker-built or carvel-planked?

In his book *Endurance*, first published by Geoffrey Bles in 1931, in a passing comment, Worsley writes on p. 89: 'The *James Caird* was double-ended and carvel-built.' In a second account, *The Great Antarctic Rescue*, published by the Folio Society in 1974, republished by Times Books in 1977, and by Norton & Co in the USA under the title *Shackleton's Boat Journey*, Worsley goes into more detail. On pp. 96–97 he states: 'She was double-ended and clinker-built to my orders in July 1914, by W & J Leslie of Coldharbour, Poplar.' He goes on to describe her construction. Unfortunately the reference to 'clinker-built' has been accepted blithely by others who have written about her since.

That she was 'carvel-planked' is obvious from a glance at the boat and the Hurley photographs confirm this. Worsley himself describes how she was caulked with wool from a muffler and as they had no pitch to seal her they used Marston's oil paints.

It is not possible that the mistake in the later books was made by Worsley. They were issued over thirty years after his death in 1943 so it must have been made in the editing.

In carvel construction the strakes, or horizontal planks used to build up the sides of a boat, butt one on top of the other. In clinker construction the strakes overlap, and this was the normal construction used in ships' lifeboats. When the strakes swell in the water, the lower edge of each plank overlaps the upper edge of the one below it and compresses it. This renders a clinker design watertight. With carvel construction the spaces between the strakes have to be caulked with oakum – teased-out hemp – which is hammered into the seams and then sealed with pitch to prevent the oakum from rotting. The two Norwegian boats, the *Dudley Docker* and the *Stancomb Wills*, were both clinker-built.

Another oddity is the remark which he makes about her build: 'She was more lightly built than is required by the Board of Trade. This made her springy and buoyant.' It still seems that he had clinker construction in mind since that comment describes more accurately the characteristics of a clinker-built boat than one of carvel design, in which the strakes are usually thicker and heavier. Why he chose this light construction is not explained. It meant that she was much lighter than the regulation ship's lifeboat carried on ocean liners and, in addition, like the other two boats, she had her ballast tanks removed before leaving the ice to make room for as much gear and stores as it was possible to carry. Macklin's observations on the packing of the *Dudley Docker* (see p. 62) give some idea of how cramped the conditions were fully loaded.

Double-ended

The *James Caird* is double-ended, that is, pointed at bow and stern, whereas the two Norwegian boats, as seen in Hurley's photograph on Elephant Island, had transom sterns – their afterends were squared off. Worsley does not explain why he chose a double-ended design. In his excellent biography *Shackleton*, Roland Huntford suggests that 'It was the new 'navigable double-ender' conceived by Colin Archer, on which the *Caird* was based.' Colin Archer was a well-known Norwegian boatbuilder of Scots descent.

On the other hand an American authority on small boats states that the double-ended design was best for a 'whaler'. (Whaling and sealing used to be the calling of a special breed of New England fishermen – witness Herman Melville's novel *Moby Dick*.) He states: 'For sea-worthiness he would have the boat double-ended, long, narrow with considerable sheer', that is, high at each end. 'Free-board may be low amidships if the ends are high, as the ends have a self-righting effect in a sea. The double-ended boat will not be pooped and the narrow stern will not force the bow under as will a wider stern.' Others maintain that a double-ended boat can be pooped. A boat is said to be 'pooped' when a following sea breaks over its stern, putting it in danger of being swamped or made unsteerable. In fact, the double-ended design is very old – the Viking ocean-going longships were double-ended.

Whalers

The term 'whaler' also creates problems. Shackleton's ship *Endurance*, a 350-ton vessel of timber construction for work in the ice, was frequently described as a 'whaler'. In his book *South* Shackleton describes her as a 'sealing vessel ... barquentine rigged'. The small boats carried by such a whaler are also called 'whalers' and so are the men who man them to harpoon whales. Thus at various times the *James Caird* is called a 'whaler', a 'lifeboat', and a 'ship's boat', while the two other boats are referred to as 'cutters'. All very confusing.

The rig of the *James Caird*

Nowhere in the various records is there a clear description of how the *James Caird* was rigged. Worsley writes: 'Her sails were: jib, standing lug and a small mizzen.' He does not specify the sail rigged on the mizzen mast. The only illustration that shows the James Caird under sail is the drawing in *South*, captioned: 'In sight of our goal, nearing South Georgia', with the note 'drawn from material supplied by the boat party'. It shows a standing lugsail on the mainmast with a loose foot, that is without a boom, but the rig on the mizzen mast cannot be seen. However, a very old mizzen sail survived in the bottom of the *James Caird* and is still there. It has a boom but the yard has disappeared. The shape, however, suggests that it was a standing lugsail, to judge from the high peak, and not a gaff rig, as shown on the model at Dulwich College.

Worsley's calculations

In his book about the voyage Worsley gives the measurements of the three boats but, for some reason unknown, omits the depth of the *James Caird* as built. The depth of a boat, that is the height of its sides, is always measured at its middle. The depths at bow and stern may also be measured and are normally higher than that at the middle. This variation is called the 'sheer'. Worsley provides two clues. At one point in his book he writes: 'She had been raised until her depth was 3 feet 7 inches.' Later he writes: 'The carpenter had built her 15 inches higher', that is when he worked on her before the christening ceremony on the ice. In his diary, Worsley records a number of calculations he made as to the boat's carrying capacity:

Before. 22.6 × 6' × 2.3 × .6 = 187 cu ft: 18 adults.

James Caird 22/11/15 after raising topsides by 3'6" so now 22'6" long × 6' deep × .6 = 292.9 cu. ft: 29 adults

Measurement after raising topsides at 45 cu. ft per ton = 6½ tons. With 1'8" freeboard less estimated boat weight at 35 cu. ft per ton = 4.6 tons. Total safe load weight = 3.8 tons deadweight.

[He refers above to raising topsides 'by' 3'6", but presumably he means 'to' 3'6".]
Dec 8. By trial. Stores 3350 lb. Men 1760 lb. Gear 180 lb.
Total: 5290 lb = 2.36 [tons] deadweight.

A question of paint

A visitor who came to see the boat in 1992 complained that she was painted – she is painted white – implying that she ought to have been displayed in natural timber. The comment surprised the author, who looked into the matter with the following results. According to the Ship Technology Department at the National

Maritime Museum, from 1900 onwards almost all ships' lifeboats in the Royal Navy and the Merchant Marine were painted white, so that one would easily be identified as a lifeboat, if it was found drifting, after a disaster at sea. The *James Caird*, built in 1914, would either have been painted white or, much less likely, varnished; it is inconceivable that she would have been left without any surface finish to protect her hull.

The various photographs taken of the boat are, of course, all in black and white. The clearest view is that taken on Elephant Island, which shows the three boats drawn up on the shore. Here the *James Caird* certainly appears to be painted white. The next close-up view chronologically is the one taken in the gardens of the Middlesex Hospital during December 1919, after she had been brought back from South Georgia. She looks very rough and weathered. There is little sign of paint, but that is understandable after her battering during the two voyages, and the rough handling she underwent on Elephant Island and South Georgia. Nor is much evident as she sits on Selfridges' roof. In the next photograph, which shows her on display at Dulwich College (see p. 151), she certainly appears to be painted white. This was probably taken during the 1920s. In 1930 she was loaned for an exhibition in Central Hall, Westminster, and in that photograph she is clearly painted white.

In the survey itemised in the next section the existence of white paint is mentioned. It is evident that the boat was painted white when she was sent from Dulwich to the Maritime Museum and it is unlikely that the authorities at the College would have had her painted if she was not already in that state when she arrived there in 1924.

A survey of the *James Caird*

The Maritime Museum carried out a survey of the boat in 1983 – see p. 162 – and three paragraphs in it refer to her state and the existence of paint on her in 1968, when she was repaired at Cory's Barge Works:

The *James Caird* is generally in good condition, the wood being sound, free from shakes and rot. Some shrinkage has occurred and the caulking is now loose. The paintwork is white with traces of red on the gunwale strake and rubbing band.

William Cory Barge Works did some work before the boat went on display and the paint stripped from the port side dates from this time. Other work which Corys carried out was obvious by the lack of paint, namely repair to the gunwale strake midships starboard side, replacement of the top three strakes, three of the thwarts and possibly the rudder which is a replacement, but is painted. [Corys supplied the rudder.]

The head of the stern has been replaced along with the metal band, this repair is noticeable because the width of the replacement part is smaller than original, but was done before the Cory repairs, as it is painted with the last coat of paint the boat received.

SOME BIOGRAPHICAL NOTES

Along with Shackleton, the following sailed on the *James Caird*. Those indicated with an asterisk made the journey to South Georgia. (Crean was on the *Stancomb Wills* for the journey to Elephant Island, while Worsley was in command of the *Dudley Docker*, the rest sailed on the *Caird* under Shackleton's command.)

Robert S. Clark 1882–1950

The biologist of the expedition, Clark was a product of the Grammar School and University of Aberdeen. He was recommended by W. S. Bruce, the Scottish explorer, who sailed the *Scotia* to explore the Weddell Sea in the Scottish expedition of 1902–04, sighting land which he named Coats Land. Clark was strong and adaptable, and a very capable member of the party. On his return from the south, he joined the Navy and served in minesweepers. After the war he joined the Scottish Fishery Board, later the Scottish Home Office Maritime Laboratory, of which he became Director.

Tom Crean 1877–1938*

An Irishman, said to be 'strong as an ox', Tom Crean served, like Wild, as an able-bodied seaman in the *Discovery* expedition, 1901–04. His abilities and experience of the Antarctic took him south again with Scott's ill-fated expedition in 1912. By then a petty officer, with PO Evans, in charge of sledge maintenance, he was a member of the second support party which, led by Lt Evans (who later became Admiral Lord Mountevans), journeyed to the polar plateau with Scott's polar party. Crean and chief stoker Lashley saved Evans' life, when he went down with scurvy. Shackleton made him Second Officer of the *Endurance*. He valued his spirit and loyalty on the ice, during the boat journey in the *James Caird* and on the march across South Georgia. After the First World War, Crean retired to the south of Ireland and opened the South Pole Inn at Anascaul in County Kerry. Although recently closed for a time, it has now been reopened and furnished with memorabilia of Tom Crean's life in the Antarctic, an appropriate memorial to a remarkable character.

Charles Green 1889–1974

'Charlie' Green joined the expedition in Buenos Aires, in search of adventure. He was hired as cook when the first choice was sacked for incompetence and proved a first-rate and resourceful one in the most appalling circumstances, particularly on the ice and afterwards on Elephant Island when supplies of food were extremely limited. In 1922, Shackleton asked him to join the *Quest* expedition.

Frank Hurley 1890–1962

An Australian who took up photography by chance at the age of seventeen, Frank Hurley quickly became fascinated by the technique and craft. He was twenty-four when Douglas Mawson (later Sir Douglas) selected him as photographer for his expedition to Antarctica in 1911. The character of the man and his expertise appealed to Shackleton and he invited him to join the *Endurance* expedition. The results of his work speak for themselves; Shackleton made full use of his films and photographs for his lectures and to illustrate his book of the expedition, *South*. Hurley made more visits to the Arctic and the Antarctic, as well as accompanying expeditions to other parts of the world and photographing the Great War.

Leonard Hussey OBE 1894–1965

A meteorologist, Hussey was also the owner of a banjo and an endless collection of songs. This factor proved a vital morale raiser on the ice and on Elephant Island, for Shackleton let him keep the banjo when surplus possessions had to be discarded to save weight.

According to Worsley: 'Many a weary evening was enlivened by Hussey's songs ... [he] was a brilliant wit, and his keen repartee was one of the few joys left to us.' On his return home Hussey was sent to North Russia with Shackleton, and in the Second World War he became a doctor in the Royal Air Force.

Reginald James 1891–1964

The physicist Reginald James was fresh from the Cavendish Laboratory and St John's College, Cambridge. Introduced by Wordie, he knew Sir Raymond Priestley, who had been with Shackleton's *Nimrod* expedition in 1907–09. Very able, but young, and out of his element, his academic upbringing made him the butt of the Boss's rough wit. He stood up to it well and turned out to be a shrewd observer of his fellows, including Shackleton, as well as being a resourceful scientist. He went on to enjoy a successful career as Professor of Physics, from 1937 to 1956, at the University of Cape Town. He was elected FRS in 1955.

Tim McCarthy 1888–1917*

An Irish AB, Shackleton described McCarthy as 'the best and most efficient of the sailors, always cheerful in the most trying of circumstances'. He proved a tower of strength on the boat journey. On his arrival back in England, he returned to the Navy and was killed in action in 1917.

Harry McNeish 1874–1930*

A Scot from Dundee, McNeish was a shipwright and ship's carpenter and the oldest member of the crew. Very capable, he was opinionated, brusque, something of a ship's lawyer who believed he 'knew his rights'. Nevertheless, he was studious and quite well read. Shackleton could not have managed without his expertise. He somehow kept the Bible presented to the ship by

Queen Alexandra which surfaced, years later, in South America and eventually found its way to the Royal Geographical Society. He died in poverty in New Zealand.

John Vincent 1879–1941*

An ex-trawler hand, Vincent was an AB known as 'Bosun'. He had earlier been made boatswain but turned out a bully – an impossible situation in a small company – and was soon demoted, but the name stuck. Shackleton took him in the *James Caird*, but although he was a strong, robust man, he turned out to be the weakest member of the crew.

Frank Wild 1874–1939

A Yorkshireman, said to be a direct descendant of Captain Cook, he had a remarkable career as an Antarctic explorer. Small, quick, strong and wiry, he had great powers of endurance and even more experience of Antarctic travel than Shackleton. He began his sea career in the Merchant service, but joined the Royal Navy in 1900 as an able-bodied seaman, became a valued member of the *Discovery* expedition from 1901 to 1904 and was awarded the Polar Medal and, some years later, a clasp. He served in the *Nimrod* expedition with Shackleton, whom he accompanied on the 'Furthest South' journey in 1908–09 as Shackleton's right-hand man to within 97 miles of the South Pole. By 1911 he was an experienced explorer, and served as an expedition leader on Mawson's Australasian Antarctic expedition. He was picked by Shackleton to be second in command of his *Endurance* expedition, and later put in charge of the party of twenty-two men, marooned on Elephant Island. Finally, after Shackleton had died at South Georgia in 1922, he took command of the *Quest* expedition. Afterwards, he retired to farm in South Africa.

James Wordie 1889–1962

A product of Glasgow Academy and University, Wordie went on to St John's College, Cambridge, became a geologist and sailed with the expedition in that capacity. He was described as 'small, dry and bespectacled' but, unlike James, his colleague from St John's, he had intended to go south and took full advantage of his opportunities. On his return he joined the Army and was commissioned into the Royal Field Artillery, serving in France. These years were a prelude to a very distinguished academic career as a scientist. He went on many other expeditions, was eventually elected Master of St John's, his old College, and was knighted in 1957 as Sir James Mann Wordie. He was elected President of the Royal Geographical Society, 1951–54 and was Chairman of the Scott Polar Research Institute Committee of Management, 1937–55.

Frank Worsley 1872–1943*

A New Zealander, Worsley served his apprenticeship in square-rigged ships on the Cape Horn run to Europe, much like Shackleton. He joined the *Endurance* expedition almost by accident and served as Master of the ship. Like Wild, he was short in stature but very strong and adventurous and used to a hard life. As a navigation specialist, he played a vital part in the success of the voyage of the *James Caird*. He was forty-two when the expedition left England, two years older than the Boss. On his return to Europe in 1917 he first talked his way into the Navy and was put in command of a 'Mystery' ship, hunting U-boats. Later, while on leave, he ran into Shackleton, who persuaded him to join him in North Russia. In 1922 he sailed again with Shackleton as Master and hydrographer in the *Quest*. Subsequently he undertook various expeditions, before returning to active service in the Second World War.

WORSLEY'S LOG OF THE BOAT JOURNEY

Frank Worsley's log of the boat journey is preserved at the Scott Polar Research Institute. It was found in a suitcaseful of papers bequeathed to the Institute by Sir James Wordie's successors.

How Worsley managed to record a readable log in the dreadful conditions of the boat journey is hard to imagine. His own description of taking a sun shot, requiring the efforts of four men, gives some idea of the difficulties he must have faced. Over the entire seventeen-day voyage of the *James Caird*, Worsley was able to make only four observations.

1916

Worsley's log

Transcribed by J. M. (later Sir James) Wordie from the original in Worsley's second work book. The following abbreviations are used:

DR   Direct Reckoning
BC   Becalmed
OMR   Overcast Moderate Rain
ZD   Zenith Distance

Cape Belsham
61° 4′ S 54° 50′ W
46° W of Wallis
54° 4′ S 39° 0′ W

	420 950
	= 661
	27
To Wallis	688
	62
To Leith Hb.	750

Monday 24 April 1916

Wild Camp for Rathing Chronometer 192/262. No observation for lat. could be obtained, and long. of Cape Belsham being only approximately known to us, allow 1 min 4 secs more slow.
= 11 mins 55 sec slow.
Took departure from Wild Camp in 'James Caird' at 12.30 p.m.
Steered NNE 8m then E 1m to a break in the stream ice, here running E and W.
Mean of courses to noon on 25th = N 64 miles.
Wind to 4 pm WNW6: to 6 am SE to N by E 5–3.
Tues to noon W 6–4.

Tuesday 25 April

N 64m from Cape Wild. 60°0′ S 54°50′ W
WSW 6 Overcast.
High NW swell and cross seas.
Chronometer 192/262
Apr 25 12m 0s slow, losing 5 secs per day.
26 12m 5s
27 12m 10s
28 12m 15
29 12m 20s
30 12m 25s

Wednesday 26 April

DR N 45° E 110 Observed 59°46′ S 50°48′ W
WSW gale, squally, cloudy, heavy seas.

Thursday 27 April

Chron. 192/262 12m 10s slow 59°46′ S 50°48′ W
Northerly gale, overcast and misty, squally.

Friday 28 April

AM: overcast. PM: cloudy.
Light NW to fresh Westerly. Overcast and misty.
High NW swell. 59°52′ S 50°0′ W. allowing 1 min 4s.
more slow for rating from Wild Camp = 50°16′.
Chron. 12m 15s slow. 59°52′ S 50°16′ W

Saturday 29 April

N 35° E 85 miles DR 24 hrs.
Fresh Westerly to WSW breeze.
Cloudy and misty. High lumpy sea.
Observed position 58°38′ S (50°0′ W?VB)
N 53° E
27° W Wallis   458
                                     90
To Leith   548

Sunday 30 April

DR N 35° E 78 miles 57°34′ S 48°36′ W
Hove to. SW by S gales
Heavy seas, overcast

Monday 1 May

DR N 0° E 30m. 57°11′ S 48°1′ W
Drift. SSW moderate gale; heavy lumpy sea;
boat lying to sea anchor; heavily iced up. Overcast.

Tuesday 2 May

N 50° E 45m 56°42′ S 46°58′ W
Strong SW by S breeze.
Overcast, lumpy sea.

Wednesday 3 May

N 55° E 85m Observed posit. 56°13' S 45°38' W
Chronometer 12m 40s slow.
(Bird Island 54°0' S 38°0' W)
To W pt Bird Island N 63° E 294m

$$\underline{53}$$

To Leith HB.   347
SW by S to W by S moderate breeze.
pm. Moderate WSW to SSE light.
Moderate Sea. southerly swell.
Blue sky, passing clouds. Fine clear weather.
Able to reduce some parts of our clothing from wet to damp.

Thursday 4 May

DR N 45° E 70m. Observed posit. 55°31' S 44°43' W
N 36° E 52m
Bird Island N 69° E 250

$$\underline{53}$$

Leith Harbour   303
SE moderate breeze
B.C. fine and clear
moderate sea

Friday 5 May

DR N 50° E 95m 54°30' S 42°36' W
SE Fresh breeze, squally, overcast.
Lumpy, confused sea and SW swell. Clear weather.
Breeze failing to 8 p.m., when shifted to NNE light and gusty.
Bird Island N 79° E 163m
Wallis N 80° E 155m
(Wallis 54°4' S 38°14' W)

Saturday 6 May

Moderate N by W gale. 54°26′ S 40°44′ W
Overcast, clear weather.
Lumpy Northerly sea.
1p.m.: Hove to. Sea too heavy to carry on.
Wallis Island N 76′ E 91m
DR N 30 E 16m to 1pm S 60 E 58m

Sunday 7 May

Observed posit: 54°38′ S 39°36′ W
NNWly gale. High Northerly sea.
Hove to till 1 a.m., then carried on again for land.
Moderate NW to N breeze and sea and high NW swell.
B.C. to 6 a.m. when it became foggy.
DR S 60° E 12m
N 70° E 28m
Bird Island N 56° E 68m
$$\frac{53}{}$$
Leith   121
Most unfavourable conditions for observations. Misty with boat jumping like a flea and no limb for early am sight. Noon lat probably correct within a 10 m limit.
(Lat proved to be correct within about 2 m. Long ditto but chronometer was much slower than I had allowed, which made us about 20m of distance further astern than observation showed.)

Monday 8 May

DR N 78′ E 90m 54°19′ S 37°2′ W

Moderate to strong NNW to WNW breezes. Overcast.

Misty and foggy with some clear intervals.

Westerly and northerly swells and lumpy, confused sea.

12.30 p.m. sighted land about 9 miles ahead.

3 p.m. stood off on starboard tack from 2m off shore. Wind N by E 5–6, O.M.R. Heavy westerly swell. Very bad lumpy confused sea. Stood off for the night. Wind WNW increasing to gale with rain, snow sleet and hail.

[There is a sketch map of the coastline at this point.]

Tuesday 9 May

Very heavy WNW – SSW gale. Rain, hail, snow and sleet. Very heavy swell and high cross sea. Nearly blown on shore; had to beat off under reefed lug, straining boat heavily. With great difficulty cleared Main Island and Annenakov [sic] Island by dark. Wind soon after coming SSW, stood W; wind and sea moderating. Heavy westerly swell.

Wednesday 10 May

7 a.m. Wind fell away very light and backed to NW. preventing us making towards Wallis Island. Stood in for King Haakon Bay for ice.

5 p.m. Landed at cove on S side of entrance to King Haakon Bay. Could not haul boat clear of surf.

Midnight. Boat broke adrift. Managed to secure her with 4 hours work and stood by her to daylight.

Thursday 11 May

Camped in small cave, dried some clothes and began to cut 'Caird' down, she being so heavy we could not handle her or haul her clear of surf. Cooked old albertross [sic]. Very good but a little tough. Moderate E to SEly breeze, clear weather, some showers.

Friday 12 May

Cutting down 'Caird'. Bringing in young albertrosses for food.
Endeavouring to dry clothes, with slight success so far, as they are
heavily soaked with salt water.
Strong SWly breeze, clear weather.

Saturday 13 May

Fresh SE breeze. Bright clear weather. Preparing 'Caird' for pulling
up to head of bay. Clothes getting moderately dry.
Brought in 17 young albertrosses: 22 to date and three old birds.
Observed: alt of sun at noon to be   17° 17′
height of eye: 12° 9′ 20″
                                      17° 26′ 20″
ZD   72° 33′ 40″
Dec   18° 22′ 53″
Lat   54° 10′ 47″
This lat. corresponds with the chart for S side of entrance to King
Haakon Bay to within 1 minute. My position should therefore
correct the drawing of the chart here, 1° to Northward.

A *JAMES CAIRD* LOG OF EVENTS

1913

May

Shackleton plans a trans-Antarctic journey.

December

The British government promises a grant of £10,000.

1914

1 January

Shackleton announces the 'Imperial Trans-Antarctic Expedition'.

June

Endurance arrives at Millwall Dock, London.
Sir James Caird gives Shackleton £24,000 towards the costs of
the expedition.

July

Worsley takes delivery of a ship's lifeboat, built to his orders, later
named the *James Caird*.

1 August

Endurance leaves Millwall dock.

3 August

She arrives at Margate to await instructions.

4 Aug

War is declared. Shackleton offers his ship and crew to the
Admiralty. The First Lord, Winston Churchill, signals him to 'Proceed'.

5 Aug

Shackleton summoned to Buckingham Palace to take leave of HM the King.

8 August

Endurance sails from Plymouth for Antarctica.

5 December

Endurance sails from South Georgia through the Weddell Sea for Vahsel Bay.

11 December

Endurance enters the pack ice.

1915

16 January

The expedition sights land; Shackleton names it Caird Coast.

19 January

Endurance is trapped in the ice.

27 October

Endurance is abandoned. Ocean Camp established on the ice.

21 November

Endurance sinks.

2–24 November

The ship's carpenter works on the 'whaler'.

26 November

The three ship's boats are christened *James Caird*, *Dudley Docker* and *Stancomb Wills*.

8 December

Trial launch of the *James Caird*.

23–29 December

Hauling the *James Caird* and the two other boats over the ice, northwards.

1916

21 January

The party in Ocean Camp drifts north of the Antarctic Circle.

26 January

Patience Camp established on the ice floes.

9 April

The three boats are launched for the journey to Elephant Island.

9–15 April

The three boats sail to Elephant Island.

15 April

The three boats land at Valentine Point, Elephant Island. The first dry land in sixteen months.

15–23 April

Preparing the *James Caird* for her voyage to South Georgia and a camp for the 22 men left behind.

24 April

Shackleton and his crew of five set sail in the *James Caird* for South Georgia. Course set, steering north. Cleared ring of pack ice.

25 April, Day 2

Keeping four-hour watches, three men to a watch. 45 miles run by daybreak.

26 April, Day 3

Hard WSW gale. Sun fix obtained. Ran 83 miles, total from starting point, 128 miles.

27 April, Day 4

Hove to in severe SW gale.

28 April, Day 5

Streamed sea anchor. Drifted 18 miles.

29 April, Day 6

WSW gale. Sun fix obtained. Ran 92 miles, total of 238 miles.

30 April, Day 7

SW by W gale. Hove to on sea anchor. Later ran 76 miles.

1 May, Day 8

Ice on boat, near capsizing, chopped off twice. Steady gale from SSW. Drifted 36 miles.

2 May, Day 9

Lost sea anchor and painter. SSW gale continued. Drifted 66 miles.

3 May, Day 10

SW gale moderated. Sun fix obtained. Hung out clothing to dry. 62 miles run, total 444 miles, over halfway.

4 May, Day 11

Moderate SE breeze. Sun fix obtained. 52 miles run, total 496 miles.

5 May, Day 12

Good SE breeze became SW gale. Ran 96 miles, total 592 miles.

6 May, Day 13

Swamped by gigantic wave. Later a sun fix placed them 100 miles from South Georgia.

7 May, Day 14

Set course for south side of South Georgia.

8 May, Day 15

Sighted Cape Demidov on South Georgia. Hard gale. Hove to 18 miles off coast.

9 May, Day 16

Mountainous westerly gale and swell. Wind rose to hurricane force. Set sail to weather Annenkov Island. Gale eased after dark, mast nearly lost.

10 May, Day 17

Wind backed to NW and ran for King Haakon Bay. Wind shifted and had to tack for four hours to enter the Bay. Landed on Cape Rosa. The voyage ended with all safe.

11 May, Day 14

Camped in small cave. *James Caird* too heavy to haul up beach so they removed decking and the two top strakes to lighten her.

12–14 May

Continued cutting down the boat and resting.

15 May

Sailed the cut-down boat to the head of the Sound, turned her over and created Peggotty Camp.

16–18 May

Resting, eating, waiting for suitable weather to cross the mountains of South Georgia. Prospected a route.

19–20 May

Shackleton, Worsley and Crean cross the snowfields, glaciers and mountains of South Georgia, covering 40 miles in 36 hours, the first to do so.

20 May

The three arrive at Stromness, welcomed by the whaling station manager, Mr Sørlle, at his villa.

20–22 May

The Norwegian steam trawler *Samson*, with Worsley on board, is sent to rescue McNeish, Vincent and McCarthy from King Haakon Bay. They bring back the *James Caird*.

23–30 May

Shackleton sails in the *Southern Sky* to rescue the 22 men left on Elephant Island. Stopped by ice barrier and heads for the Falklands.

31 May

They arrive at Port Stanley in the Falklands. Cable news of their survival to the King in London.

10 June

Shackleton makes a second attempt in Uruguayan trawler *Instituto de Pesca No 1* but fails to penetrate ice. Travels to Punta Arenas in Chile.

12 July

Shackleton makes a third attempt in the schooner *Emma* but fails again, returning to Port Stanley.

25 August

Shackleton returns to Punta Arenas and makes his fourth attempt in the steam trawler *Yelcho*, loaned by the Chilean government with a crew of Chilean Navy volunteers.

30 August

They penetrate the ice, and rescue the 22 castaways, who are all safe and well.

3 September

Shackleton and his men arrive at Punta Arenas to a great welcome. Shackleton then travels via San Francisco and New Zealand to collect the party in the *Aurora* who are awaiting his arrival from the South Pole, at McMurdo Sound.

1919

December

The *James Caird* arrives at Birkenhead from South Georgia in the *Woodville* or more likely the *Orwell* (see p. 212, endnote 17). She is brought to London on a railway truck by Worsley and Stenhouse, Captain of *Aurora*.

15 December

The *James Caird* is placed in the gardens of the Middlesex Hospital to collect money for the hospital appeal fund.

19 December

The *James Caird* is taken to the Royal Albert Hall for Shackleton's lecture on the expedition and is returned to Middlesex Hospital afterwards.

1920

14 February

The *James Caird* is displayed on the roof of Selfridges department store near the Marble Arch.

1921

The *James Caird* is moved to Ely Place, at Frant, the home of John Quiller Rowett, a school friend of Shackleton's.

17 September

Shackleton sails south on his fourth expedition to the Antarctic, financed by Rowett and Becker.

1922

5 January

Shackleton dies of a heart attack at Grytviken, South Georgia. The body is sent to Montevideo, but is returned to Grytviken at his wife's request.

2 March

A memorial service is held in St Paul's Cathedral, London.

5 March

Shackleton is buried in the Norwegian cemetery at Grytviken, South Georgia.

The Alleyn Club, comprising former pupils of Dulwich College, where Shackleton went to school, opens an appeal for a Shackleton Memorial.

2 July

J. Q. Rowett offers to give the *James Caird* to Dulwich College as a memorial. The offer is accepted.

1924

11 April

The *James Caird* is installed at Dulwich College.

1928

15 February

A granite headstone brought from England is installed over Shackleton's grave at Grytviken at a special service in English and Norwegian to replace the existing wooden one.

1930

2–25 July

The *James Caird* is loaned to the British Polar Exhibition in Central Hall, Westminster.

1944

10 July

A VI flying bomb destroys nearby buildings at Dulwich College but the *James Caird* survives.

1967

May

The *James Caird* is sent on temporary loan to the National Maritime Museum at Greenwich.

1968

The *James Caird* restored and rigged and put on display in the Neptune Hall.

1969

December

Neptune Hall closed for repair and the *James Caird* is removed and put in store.

1969–1974

The *James Caird* remains in the Museum's store.

1970

July

A model of the boat is installed at Dulwich College.

1974

May

The *James Caird*, unrigged, displayed in the Half-Deck, in the Museum's East Wing.

9 May

The centenary of Shackleton's birth (15 February 1874) is celebrated in the Half-Deck by Lord Shackleton and others.

30 May

The Children's Gallery and the Half-Deck opened officially by Princess Anne.

1982

Christopher Ralling writes and produces his much-acclaimed four-part television film *Shackleton*. A book with a selection of Shackleton's writings followed.

1986

October

The Museum's East Wing is closed and the *James Caird* returned to Dulwich College.

1989

30 August

The *James Caird* installed in a special display in the North Cloister at Dulwich.

12 September

Lord Shackleton, son of the explorer, opens a new Shackleton Building and visits the *James Caird*, now the Shackleton memorial.

1993

24 December

Trevor Potts embarks with three colleagues on his 'In the Wake of Shackleton' expedition, the first ever re-enaction attempted, without support ship, arriving at South Georgia on 5 January 1994, but landing on the North East Coast.

1994

5–16 January

The *James Caird* on display at the London International Boat Show at Earls Court, London.

19 May

The James Caird Society inaugurated at a meeting held at Dulwich College.

22 September

Lord Shackleton KG, OBE, FRS, PC, Life President of The James Caird Society, dies.

28 October

The first James Caird Society meeting at Dulwich College. Trevor Potts gives a lecture on his 'In the Wake of Shackleton' expedition when, with three companions, he repeated the famous boat journey during December 1993 and January 1994.

1995

16 January

The James Caird Society holds a joint meeting with the Royal Geographical Society in the latter's Lecture Hall, when Trevor Potts repeats the lecture on his 'In the Wake of Shackleton' expedition to a packed audience.

25 January

A Memorial Service held in Westminster Abbey to the memory of the late Lord Shackleton. Tribute given by Lord Jellicoe.

19 May

James Caird Society meeting at Dulwich College with a lecture by Captain Alan Phillips, RN, Commander of HMS *Endurance*, about his last patrol in the Weddell Sea.

5 October

James Caird Society meeting, including the first AGM, followed by the Leonard Hussey Lecture, given by Geoffrey Selley, at Dulwich College.

1996

10 May

A James Caird Society meeting celebrates the 80th anniversary of Shackleton's landing on South Georgia, 10 May 1916.
A re-enactment of the expedition is presented by Harding Dunnett, Angus Erskine, Keith Shackleton, Michael Gilkes and Giles Bergel, the explorer's great-grandson.

1997

January–February

The South Áris Expedition, led by Frank Nugent, attempts the sea crossing from Elephant Island to South Georgia but their vessel, the *Tom Crean*, is abandoned on 26 January after a violent force 10 gale. However, the party continues in the support ship *Pelagic* and from 9 February makes a successful crossing of South Georgia in just 48 hours. www.iol.ie/~stharis/index.htm

The *James Caird* is the major artifact displayed at the exhibition 'Arktis-Antarktis', mounted at the Bundeskunsthalle, Bonn, Germany. The exhibition runs until mid-April 1998 and attracts massive interest.

1999

The *James Caird* is displayed at the much-visited and highly influential Shackleton exhibition at the American Museum of Natural History, New York. The James Caird Society is represented by the President, Chairman and Hon. Secretary. The exhibition continued to the Peabody Essex Museum, Salem, near Boston, from June to September 2000, though by then the boat had returned to England.

2000

The exhibition 'South – The Race to the Pole' is launched at the National Maritime Museum in Greenwich. It is so successful that its run is extended to 2001.

The much-admired exhibition 'Shackleton, The Antarctic and *Endurance*', curated by Dr Jan Piggott, is displayed at Dulwich College from 31 October 2000 to 25 February, 2001, with the *James Caird* as its centrepiece.

2001

Shackleton's Antarctic Adventure, a magnificent film in large-scale IMAX format, narrated by Kevin Spacey, is launched. There was a celebration and well-attended first showing at the London IMAX theatre, Waterloo for members of The James Caird Society, at which HRH Princess Anne was guest of honour.

The *Antarctic Symphony* by Sir Peter Maxwell Davies is premiered at the Royal Festival Hall in London on 6 May.

The Ernest Shackleton Autumn School is launched on 26 October at the Athy Heritage Centre, close to where Shackleton was born. It immediately established itself as a major occasion in the Shackleton calendar, and its full programme of lectures continues to be a major resource for the advancement of Shackleton research.

2002

The Hon. Alexandra Shackleton is in heavy demand as she continues both to represent The James Caird Society and to honour her grandfather's memory at major events across the world, including Australia, New Zealand, Spain, the United States and South America, as well as Antarctica on several occasions.

Kenneth Branagh stars as Ernest Shackleton in Charles Sturridge's four-part TV film *Shackleton*, for which both actor and producer earn many accolades. Some two years earlier, Harding Dunnett had assisted in showing Branagh the *James Caird* at Dulwich.

2004

The Museum of New Zealand Te Papa Tongarewa, Wellington, New Zealand, mounts the major exhibition 'Antarctic Heroes: The Race to the South Pole', running from 19 May to 26 October. The *James Caird* is specially loaned to the exhibition by Dulwich College, offering New Zealanders a rare chance of seeing Shackleton's historic vessel.

2006

The *James Caird* is the central feature of the '*Endurance* and Survival' exhibition, which runs at Discovery Key, Falmouth in Cornwall from 11 February to January 2007.

2007

A major exhibition entitled '*Atrapados en el Hielo* – Trapped in the Ice: Shackleton's Legendary Antarctic Exhibition' opened in Barcelona and toured to many venues across Spain until 2009. The Hon. Alexandra Shackleton, President of The James Caird Society, was honoured guest at the opening.

2008

The Matrix Shackleton Centenary Expedition, including three descendants or relations of the original *Nimrod* party members, and led by Lt Colonel Henry Worsley, completes the journey of the original *Nimrod* southern party and in 2009 arrives at the South Pole, a century after Shackleton decided to turn back. www.shackletoncentenary.org

2011

The 90-minute film *Shackleton's Captain*, a tribute to Ernest Shackleton's tireless skipper and supreme navigator, Frank Worsley, produced by James Heyward of Making Movies in collaboration with Gebrueder Beetz in Germany, is launched.

2012

The Quest for Frank Wild, a film by Angie Butler retelling the story of this neglected Polar hero and explaining how his remains were tracked down in Johannesburg, and conveyed to South Georgia so they could be buried next to Shackleton, drew much attention and interest. Angie Butler lectured to the Society at Dulwich and there is an accompanying book. http://questforfrankwild.com

2013

In their boat the *Alexandra Shackleton*, the Shackleton Epic Expedition, led by Tim Jarvis AM FRGS, and consisting of five British and Australian members, becomes the first authentically to re-enact Shackleton's dangerous crossing from Elephant Island to South Georgia, and achieves the 'double' by completing the mountain crossing made from King Haakon Bay by Shackleton, Worsley and Crean.

2014

The Shackleton Endurance Exhibition, with many photos and artifacts, runs at the Ferry Terminal Building, Dun Laoghaire, Ireland till August 2015. This much-travelled exhibition was originally curated by the American Museum of Natural History, New York.

2015

The James Caird Society celebrates its 21st birthday with a special lunch party aboard the HQS *Wellington*, moored off Temple Pier in Central London.

ENDNOTES

1 Ross named McMurdo Sound after the First Lieutenant in the *Terror*.

2 A quote from Ann Savours' book: *The Voyages of the Discovery*, Virgin Books, 1992, p. 30.

3 Sir James Wordie, geologist in the *Endurance* expedition, in an article in the Geographical Magazine, 1922.

4 When Sir Vivian Fuchs, leading the Commonwealth Trans-Antarctic Expedition 1955–58, completed the same journey in 1958, using Sno-cats and tractors, and aircraft for reconnaissance, they actually covered 2,158 miles in 99 days, from their Weddell Sea base to McMurdo Sound, via the South Pole.

5 *Endurance* by Frank Worsley, Geoffrey Bles, 1931.

6 There was a fourth boat – a motor boat – which Worsley mentions in his book *Endurance* (*ibid.*) when it was used to tow a dead and stinking whale to leeward of the ship. *Endurance* was at Grytviken, waiting to sail south. The boat hangs from the davits of the wrecked ship, see photo on p. 36.

7 In fact she was carvel-built. How this mistake came about is discussed in Part III p. 180.

8 This is the inside measurement. She was 23 feet 6 inches overall. See p. 183 for more details.

9 See Part IV, pp. 186–190 for biographical notes.

10 *South*, 1919, Heinemann p. 124.

11 Dr A. H. Macklin's account appears in *Shackleton*, the biography by Margery and James Fisher, 1957, Barrie, p. 367.

12 William Bakewell had been stranded when his former ship had run aground and, with his friend, Percy Blackborow, applied to join *Endurance* in Buenos Aires, to replace two members of the crew whom Shackleton had dismissed from the ship on its arrival from England. Shackleton liked the look of Bakewell and took him on, unaware that he was, in fact a United Stated citizen, born in Illinois. He thought he had a better chance of being accepted for an 'Imperial' expedition if he posed as a Canadian. Blackborow was turned down as too young. With the aid of How, another AB, Bakewell smuggled the younger man aboard, hid him in a cupboard where he was not discovered until the ship was at sea. Hauled before Shackleton he was told that, if the food ran out, he would be the first to be eaten. Appropriately, he was signed on as steward. These facts came to light only recently when John Blackborow, a grandson of the stowaway, sent the author an article, published in *Marguette Monthly*, an American magazine, in 1993, in which a reporter disclosed that a respected local farmer named Bakewell, living in Skandia, Michigan, had once taken part in the *Endurance* expedition with Shackleton.

13 An extract from their biography *Shackleton*, by Margery and James Fisher, Barrie, 1957.

14 Shackleton spells his name 'McCarthy'.

15 The author has learned from a Norwegian source that the two 'boys' were, in fact, girls.

16 *Argonauts of the South*. Frank Hurley, 1925, Putnam, p. 248.

17 Worsley states this in his book *Shackleton's Boat Journey*. However, the London newspaper, the *Daily Graphic*, in its issue for 17 December 1919, writes that 'she was lying in a boatyard in Birkenhead'. Birkenhead is in the Wirral, across the Mersey estuary from Liverpool. Nearby is Port Sunlight, where Lever Bros manufactured soap. According to Lloyds List for 5 December 1919 the *Woodville* arrived from South Georgia at Liverpool on that day,

presumably with a cargo of whale oil in barrels. There can be little doubt that she brought the *James Caird* as deck cargo. The Norwegians presumably preserved her with care, and doubtless Shackleton arranged her transportation. Three years later the *Woodville* was to bear Shackleton's body to South Georgia for burial. (It has been pointed out by Bob Burton that a more likely candidate is the *Orwell*, on which Captain Thom brought McNeish, McCarthy and Vincent to Liverpool.)

18 'OA' stands for 'Old Alleynian', the name given to former pupils of Dulwich College.

19 A mistake for *Endurance*.

20 According to Geoffrey Hattersley-Smith, the erection of the first cross was entrusted to George Vibert Douglas, a Canadian, who served with Shackleton as geologist on the *Quest* expedition. He chose Hope Point at the northern entrance of King Edward Cove, Grytviken, for a white cross surmounting a cairn. It was sited to face the South Magnetic Pole because this had been located during the *Nimrod* expedition.

21 Shackleton had preserved the flyleaf of the Bible with Queen Alexandra's message inscribed on it, the 2nd Psalm and pages from the Book of Job, but jettisoned the rest. McNeish regarded this as unlucky, and rescued the rest of the Bible, which is now in the possession of the Royal Geographical Society.

22 Originally the name of Shackleton's ship was given as *Endeavour*, which had to be erased and corrected. Grytyiken is a misspelling, which remained unnoticed until recently.

23 1985, Hodder & Stoughton.

INDEX

Note: numbers in **bold italics** denote illustrations

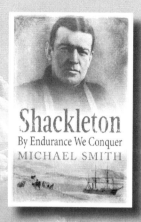

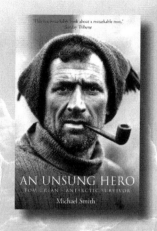

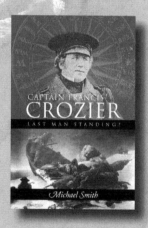

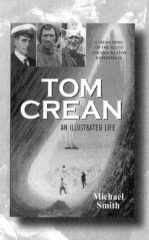

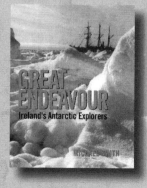

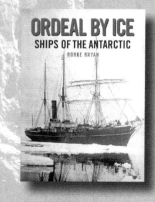